DECISION MAKING
AND FAMILY SOCIA

Perspectives on Children's
Participation

Clive Diaz

Foreword by Louise Tickle

P

First published in Great Britain in 2020 by

Policy Press
University of Bristol
1-9 Old Park Hill
Bristol
BS2 8BB
UK
t: +44 (0)117 954 5940
pp-info@bristol.ac.uk
www.policypress.co.uk

British Library Cataloguing in Publication Data
A catalogue record for this book is available from the British Library

ISBN 978-1-4473-5444-4 hardback
ISBN 978-1-4473-5445-1 paperback
ISBN 978-1-4473-5447-5 ePdf
ISBN 978-1-4473-5448-2 ePub

The rights of Clive Diaz and Lorna Stabler to be identified as authors of this work has been asserted by them in accordance with the Copyright, Designs and Patents Act 1988.

Cover design by Robin Hawes
Front cover image: iStock-1055880976

Contents

List of figures

List of abbreviations

ADCS	Association of Directors of Children's Services
BAAF	British Association of Adoption and Fostering
BASW	British Association of Social Workers
CiC	Child in Care
DfE	Department for Education
DfES	Department for Education and Skills
DoH	Department of Health
HCPC	Health and Care Professions Council
IRO	Independent Reviewing Officer
LA	Local Authority
NSPCC	National Society for the Prevention of Cruelty to Children
PEP	Personal Education Plan
SM	Senior Manager
SW	Social Worker
UNCRC	United Nations Convention on the Rights of the Child

Notes on the authors

Clive Diaz is a research associate at Children's Social Care Research and Development Centre (CASCADE), Cardiff University. He is an experienced lecturer and has worked for many years as a social worker and independent reviewing officer and as a principal social worker for two local authorities. Diaz is particularly interested in carrying out research to gain children's and parent's perspectives of social work services. He has published a number of journal articles which have considered the way in which parents and children are involved in decision making when they have had social work involvement.

Lorna Stabler is a research associate working in Children's Social Care Research at Cardiff University. She has undertaken a number of projects in social work research, working directly with social workers, families, young people and children and drawing together international literature on interventions to evaluate social work practice and its potential to improve the lives of families. The uniting aim of these projects has been to improve service delivery for families, young people and children that need social welfare support.

She is particularly keen to understand and incorporate the lived experience of those who have experienced services into service development, implementation and evaluation by taking a participatory approach to research. Stabler herself grew up in foster care and so brings this perspective to her writing and research.

She was selected as Winston Churchill Memorial Fellow in 2019, which reflects her commitment to learning from the experiences of people from different cultures and social environments across the globe.

Acknowledgements

Firstly I would like to thank Lorna Stabler for writing Chapter 2 and Louise Tickle for writing the foreword. Alyson Rees and Dawn Mannay have been patient and supportive while I carried out some of the research in this book for my doctoral thesis. I am grateful to Sophie Hallett for suggesting I write this book and for putting me in touch with Policy Press. I would also like to thank Mark Chesterman for his encouragement to get on with this research and Donna Neil and Nigel Thomas for their assistance with my research in recent years. I would also like to thank colleagues at Cardiff University including Donald Forrester, Jonathan Scourfield, Louise Roberts, Daniel Burrows and David Wilkens.

My thanks also extend to all the young people and families who have worked with social workers, students, social workers, academics and other professionals whom I talked to about meaningful participation over the last ten years.

I am indebted to the young people, social workers, independent reviewing officers and senior managers who gave me their valuable time as part of this research project.

I would like to recognise my friend Tricia Aylward for her advice and support during this research project and Lee Mannion, Lucie Boase, Alex Gude, Abby Hennessey, Katie Campbell, Natasha Wilson and Hannah Thompson for their feedback. I would like to thank Robin Gordon Brown for his support over the last 19 years; there is no way I would have ever written this book without him and I am eternally grateful. I would also like to thank Lee Mannion for giving me advice and feedback on the book proposal; Sarah Bird, my editor at Policy Press, who has been very supportive throughout this process; and Amelia Watts-Jones, also from Policy Press.

Finally, I would like to show my appreciation to my family for their support and love during this time. My mother has been enormously supportive and gave me very helpful feedback and was always willing to help with looking after Emilio. My father gave me some useful advice along the way. My partner Hayley helped both with this research and generally with day-to-day life. Lastly, I would like to thank my son Emilio and daughter Luna for bringing so much joy to my life.

Foreword

Louise Tickle

Any half-decent parent listens to their children. They tease out their concerns, think about their emotional needs. They ask their child what they want and try to help them work out their preferences.

Some decision making – 'I want to have a sleepover' – will be entirely driven by what children tell parents they want. Before making other, bigger choices that affect their children's lives parents will think deeply about a number of factors that could influence the long-term outcome, including some that a child will not have considered for themselves. Yes, of course they will always have to weigh their child's interests and desires against competing priorities, such as the impact on their other children or family finances, before deciding on a course of action. And yes, the outcome might not please a child – indeed they might be angry and resistant – but typically parents will have actively elicited their child's opinion and taken it into account. As a result, over time, that child comes to realise that while their views don't always win out, their opinions, needs and desires can and do influence what happens. They have agency in their own lives. And so they come to understand that they matter.

Thinking about their child's needs and wants underscores parents' lives from the moment a baby is born. Parents spend untold time and mental energy thinking about and discussing their children: for parents in a couple it's often a standing joke that a night out almost invariably ends up in conversation about their kids: what is their eldest troubled by, what's the best way to help the one who's having a wobble? That conversation will be informed by a deep, nuanced knowledge of their children and by the ongoing conversations they have had with their child that give parents insight into how they're feeling. A child who lives at home will be overwhelmingly likely to have at least one adult in their family who spends a substantial part of their waking life – and sometimes sleepless nights – thinking about their needs, considering what they want, managing as sensitively as possible competing family interests, and weighing up what to do for the best. Certainly parents don't always get it right, but the focus on children by most parents is intense, enquiring, committed, flexible – and enduring.

Not so when children are in the care of the state. This book explores, through research with children in care and professionals, just how little children's views count for when it comes to the operational reality of their 'corporate parent'. Children interviewed for this research describe how they are often not meaningfully involved in planning for their lives in care, let alone actively asked what they want. Important statutory review meetings are scheduled to suit the priorities of professionals, with little thought for the needs of the child who is, supposedly, the entire reason for the meeting; an example that speaks volumes is that of a child who was called to attend such a meeting on their birthday. Where's the care in that?

But the professionals don't always see things that way. This research also shows, in their own words, the desensitisation of many of those who work in the children's social care system to the urgent need of children to be involved in shaping their own lives. It's hardly surprising, given social work caseloads of up to 40, social worker burnout, the constant flux of inexperienced social workers into and then out of the system, and the constant pressures of meeting statutory targets. Families know their members intimately. They care about those they love. But systems do not, and can end up, often but not always unconsciously, serving their own needs, rather than those of the people they have been set up to protect.

Could it be different? As with anything in life, only if we first bring consciousness to our failings – and then decide we care enough to change. Through identifying uncomfortable truths about how the child protection system does not always care for those it aims to protect, this research enables people to take that first step. Whether the second is taken depends on how much those in the system care enough to challenge its failings – and their own.

Introduction

This book presents new research on how parents and children participate in decision making when childcare social workers (SWs) are involved. Two specific meetings where such decision making occurs – Child Protection Conferences and Child in Care reviews – are considered in depth.

A Child in Care (CiC) review is a key meeting that considers the care plan for a child or young person in care; the person in care should play a meaningful role in the decision making that takes place at the meeting. CiC reviews are held one month after a child comes into care or changes placement, at three months and then at six-monthly intervals. In the past, reviews were chaired by a team manager; however, since 2002 the role of Independent Reviewing Officer (IRO) has been introduced to chair this meeting and provide independent oversight and scrutiny of the care plan.

A Child Protection Conference is a meeting to 'review whether the child is continuing to suffer or is likely to suffer significant harm and review developmental progress against child protection plan outcomes' (*Working Together*, DfE, 2018, p 46). When children are in care or subject to a Child Protection Plan, families are generally obliged to work with child and family SWs. It is therefore important to explore how this working relationship is experienced in practice and whether children, young people and their families feel they can contribute to decision-making processes relating to their lives.

Enabling SWs to work more effectively with families, and in particular ensuring children have a voice, is a subject which is currently attracting considerable attention. The child protection system, and more specifically the means by which children are safeguarded by SWs and other key professionals, is also of great interest to both the public and the media. As a former SW, it is my strong view that unless we listen to – and, wherever possible, act upon – the views of children and parents, it is very difficult to safeguard them, uphold and protect their rights, and offer them an effective service.

This subject area has been of interest to me since I attended my first CiC review as a student SW in 2005, and this initial interest continued to develop during my early years as a social work practitioner. Since becoming an IRO/Child Protection Chair in 2010 and an IRO manager in 2012, my interest in the effectiveness of review meetings and Child Protection Conferences has grown still further. I am particularly interested in how young people and their families can be encouraged to meaningfully participate in decision making.

This book will consider how ten years of austerity has impacted on the child protection system from the perspective of children, families, SWs and senior managers (SMs). It will discuss the issue in the contexts of both policy and practice. In particular, it will focus on how current practice often leads to children and parents feeling oppressed and excluded from decision-making processes relating to their lives. This text is based on original empirical research involving interviews with multiple stakeholders across two local authorities (LAs) in England, comprising children (n=75), parents (n=52), SWs (n=11), IROs (n=8) and SMs (n=7). In LA 1, interviews were carried out with 25 children in care, 25 children subject to a Child Protection Plan at the time of the interview and 30 parents of the children who were subject to a Child Protection Plan. In LA 2, 10 children in care, 15 children subject to a Child Protection Plan and 22 of their parents were interviewed. Furthermore, in Local Authority Two, 11 SWs, 8 IROs and 7 SMs were interviewed.

The two LAs in this study were chosen in part because of the stark differences between them: one is small and relatively wealthy, with a very good Ofsted report, while the other is a much larger shire county with pockets of both great wealth and poverty, which Ofsted has deemed 'Requiring Improvement' for children in care. The particular research sites were also selected since I had been given assured access to participants via the gatekeepers at these LAs, and had established a high level of trust and familiarity with staff there.

There are risks when researchers are too familiar with the setting and subject which they are researching. Geer (1964) highlights the difficulties of studying everyday familiar settings and the implicit risk that the researcher may not notice anything exceptional or strange if they are familiar with the setting they are researching. Becker (1971, p 10) argues that it takes a great deal of imagination and willpower by the researcher to ensure that they are not just seeing things that are 'conventionally there to be seen'. Morris et al (2015) are among the few scholars in social work who have considered the issue of familiarity; they highlight the potential risk of researching a subject matter you are very familiar with alongside the possible issue of almost colluding with your participants as you share a common knowledge.

As an experienced SW, it was essential that I tried to make the subject of my research 'strange' even though it was, in fact, extremely familiar. Had I not been able to achieve this, I would have been less able to critically reflect on the practice setting where my research took place, undermining the validity of my findings. Shaw and Gould (2001) argue that, when carrying out qualitative research, the researcher is the main 'instrument of the study'; it is therefore essential that the researcher is reflective and aware of the impact of the 'self' when conducting fieldwork. If they are overly familiar with the subject matter they are researching and perceive themselves to be an expert, they are less likely to be able to reflect on their subject matter and therefore less able to carry out meaningful research.

This text will provide an overview of the enablers of and barriers to 'meaningful participation' by parents and children in meetings and decisions which will potentially have a major impact on their lives. If professionals enable children and young people to effectively participate in decision making, it can have a positive impact on their self-esteem and confidence. In turn, this may help increase resilience, thus improving life chances and outcomes as they transition into adulthood (Gilligan, 2004). Research shows that participation can be seen as a protective factor for vulnerable children and young people, leading to increased levels of confidence, self-efficacy and self-worth (Dickens et al, 2015).

I will highlight inherent problems in the child protection system and the impact these have upon children, young people, parents and professionals. I will discuss how the retention crisis in childcare social work, which sees SWs leaving their roles on average within two years of commencing them, impacts significantly on the service that vulnerable children and families receive and in turn their ability to build up meaningful trusting relationships with their SWs.

The research undertaken within the two LAs found evidence of SMs in children's social care being 'wilfully blind' of the both poor and oppressive practice of not involving children or families in decision making. Wilful blindness has been defined as occurring when 'senior managers remain unseeing in situations where they could know, and should know, but don't know because it makes them feel better not to know' (Heffernan, 2014, p 11). A good example of this is that in one of the LAs in which we carried out research, the children and young people we interviewed had a demonstrably better understanding of the pressures that SWs faced than SMs. Moreover, the parents who were interviewed reported that they often felt a mixture of anger and sympathy for their SWs who seemed 'tired, burned out and stressed'. This ties in with Forrester's notion of 'zombie social work' which is 'characterised by a purposelessness that leaves worker and family confused about what is happening' (2016, p 12).

Methodological approach

I wanted to gain an understanding of participants' experiences of decision making and in particular Child Protection Conferences and CiC reviews. A qualitative approach enables in-depth understanding of the topic and a nuanced understanding of participants' views (Thomas, 2003). This approach enabled me to explore children's, young people's and professionals' experiences of CiC reviews and Child Protection Conferences and how they felt about these meetings. Further, I was able to explore the potential barriers that exist in terms of maximising children's participation. Qualitative research is widely used in social work research and has been described as a methodological approach that 'fits' with social work practice (Shaw and Gould, 2001). For Denzin and Lincoln (2011, p 3), qualitative research is 'a situated activity that locates the observer in the world. It consists of a set of interpretative material practices that make the world visible.' It was therefore essential that I gained the perspectives of children and families who came into contact with services and the professionals who were either directly delivering services or overseeing service delivery.

Sampling

Research participants were selected via purposive sampling. There are certain known ethical issues relating to the fairness of purposive sampling, since only some children and professionals are given the opportunity to express their views (Hill, 2006). However, it would have been unrealistic to interview all children and families in those LAs, as well as all of their SWs and IROs.

In order to capture the views of children and young people at different stages of the care system, those who were selected to be interviewed for this study ranged in age from 8 to 17. The only exclusion criteria were children under the age of 8, since having reflected on the ethics of research with participants under the age of 8, particularly relating to gaining informed consent, I found that best practice suggested that their inclusion would be prohibitively challenging (Holland et al, 2010).

The United Nations Convention on the Rights of the Child (UNCRC) (1989) has played an important role in pre-empting the development of more participatory research with children (Mannay, 2016). The Convention sets out the rights for all children 'to express views in all decisions that affect them'. In that sense the CiC review is clearly an example of a meeting that should encourage children to play a leading role in any decisions that are taken at this forum. Likewise the Convention clearly supports the view that it is essential that research is carried out 'with' rather than 'about' children (MacNaughton et al, 2007).

Why is it important to consider participation by children and young people?

The UNCRC (1989) provides a useful starting point when considering the importance of participation for children.

The Convention's articles include:

Article 3: The best interests of the child must be the priority in all decisions and actions that affect children.

Article 12: Every child has the right to express their views, feelings and wishes in all matters affecting them and to have their views considered and taken seriously.

Article 13: Every child must be free to express their thoughts and opinions and to access all kinds of information, as long as it is within the law.

Article 20: If a child cannot be looked after by their immediate family, the government must give them special protection and assistance. This includes making sure the child is provided with alternative care that is continuous and respects the child's culture, language and religion.

Article 25: If a child has been placed away from home for the purpose of care or protection (for example, with a foster family or in hospital), they have the right to a regular review of their treatment, the way they are cared for and their wider circumstances.

Social work values also provide a useful grounding. SWs in England are bound by a Code of Ethics (BASW, 2015) that emphasises the importance of anti-oppressive practice. In Wales, a similar Code of Professional Practice for Social Care Workers is followed. These codes require SWs to respect service-user autonomy and promote self-determination. Furthermore, social work training and continued post-qualifying development continues to assess SWs' ability to encourage and facilitate participation (Social Care Wales, 2017). This is recognised as most pertinent for children in care, who face greater disadvantage and for whom the ability to communicate needs, wishes and feelings are particularly important (Thomas and O'Kane, 1999).

In the last decade greater emphasis has been placed on service-user involvement within services (Cowden, 2012). Following the Victoria Climbié Inquiry in 2001, Lord Laming recommended that a Children's Commissioner be appointed. Such a position was established in Wales the same year, with the Children's Commissioner for England following in 2005. The remit of both commissioners includes understanding what children and young people think about issues that affect them and encouraging decision makers to always take their best interests into account. In 2013, the Department for Education (DfE) made a policy commitment to improving outcomes for young people. A significant aspect of this is ensuring that young people have opportunities to participate in decisions that affect them (DfE, 2013a). Decisions about children in care and changes to their care plan are made at CiC reviews, meaning that the importance of a child's participation in this process is paramount. The aim of the review is to ensure the child's welfare is promoted for the period that they are in care (DfES, 2010).

Although there have been positive steps forward in young people's involvement, it has been argued that:

> The key issue is not participation or no participation, but whether adults are genuinely attentive and responsive to young people's perspectives, and aware of the plurality and polyphony of their voices. (Hartas and Lindsay, 2011, p 131)

The extent to which a child or young person's views are taken into consideration is the result of a wide range of factors. In Chapter 2, a discussion of theories of participation will consider these issues further.

A system under strain

Children's social work services in England and Wales are under a great deal of pressure. Since 2008 there has been a 70 per cent increase in the numbers of children subject to Child Protection Plans and a 145 per cent increase in care proceedings (DfE, 2016). During the same period, LAs have faced cuts in funding of between 35 and 40 per cent. The numbers of children in care are also rising. As of March 2017, there were 72,670 children in care in England and 5,954 children in care in Wales, marking an 8 per cent increase for England and a 4 per cent increase for Wales since 2012.

The increase in demand has generally led to higher caseloads and more complex work for SWs to manage, although there is a great deal of inconsistency across the country. Average caseloads in Kensington and Chelsea (one of only two LAs that have achieved an Outstanding grade under the previous Ofsted inspection framework) are in the region of eight children per SW. A report in 2011 found that SWs in 5 LAs were managing an average of between 30 and 40 cases (Higgs, 2011) and in 2016 Ofsted identified 14 LAs as having persistently high caseloads (Ofsted, 2017). Statistics also illustrate that there are substantial variations between LAs and the ways in which they manage childcare work. Figures from the DfE (2014) showed that 1 child in 500 in Wokingham or Richmond upon Thames was 'looked after', compared with 1 child in 65 in Blackpool or 1 child in 75 in Wolverhampton. In Torfaen in Wales 1 child in 52 is in care; this figure has tripled in the last 15 years. Regional differences are also startling: over 80 children per 10,000 of the population are 'looked after' in the North East and 90 children per 10,000 in Wales. By contrast, only around 50 children per 10,000 are 'looked after' in London, the South East and the South West (Featherstone et al, 2014). It would appear that there are differences too in the way that child protection cases are managed in different areas of the country and by different LAs, although some of the differences can no doubt be attributed to regional disparities in wealth (Bywaters and Brady, 2017). This raises public policy questions as to how the local and national governments work to ensure that professionals perform their duties in a fair way with families where there are child protection concerns (Diaz and Drewery, 2016; Tickle, 2018).

The pressured work environment is one of the reasons why SWs leave frontline child protection practice, on average, just two to three years after qualifying (Bowyer and Roe, 2015). This means that many LAs have a very inexperienced workforce, and it is not uncommon for half of the SWs in a LA frontline team to have less than two years of post-qualifying experience. This contributes to a very challenging climate for SWs to work alongside vulnerable families and is compounded by newly qualified SWs feeling that they have to cut their teeth by doing child protection work (Munro, 2016). Munro offered an interesting reflection on how this differed 30–40 years ago:

> Social work with child protection used to be the elite part of social work. Back in the 1980s and 90s it was very difficult to get a job in child protection because when people got one they stayed there. The teams around London would've been full of people who had been in post for years and years. (Munro, 2016, p 14)

By its very nature, the emotionally demanding work undertaken by SWs has an impact on their ability to continue working with vulnerable children and adults on a long-term basis (Diaz et al, 2018). Working on a regular basis with adults and families who live chaotic lives characterised by abuse and neglect can lead to vicarious trauma (Rosenbloom et al, 1995). A National Society for the Prevention of Cruelty to Children (NSPCC) study that considered the emotional damage caused by working with families in crisis for an extended period concluded the following:

> If the emotional consequences of this work are not mitigated they will affect a professional's wellbeing as well as their ability to work effectively. Vicarious trauma can accumulate over a long period of time or it can be brought about by one-off traumatic events. (NSPCC, 2013a)

The threat of compassion fatigue, vicarious trauma and burnout is a risk to SWs and it is essential that the system is able to protect them as far as is possible (Morrison, 2005; Gibbs et al, 2009; Carpenter et al 2013).

A further complication is the high rates of SWs who carry out agency work. A recent *Guardian* report showed that in several LAs, over 30 per cent of their SWs are agency staff, which often means that they leave at short notice and only complete short-term contracts, which again impacts on the consistency of service for families.

My professional experience in recent years is that there has been a move towards agency work by a number of SWs. In terms of the national picture, Community Care (2015) suggested that:

> Social workers are making an exodus to agency work in an attempt to gain some control over their lives. A *Community Care* investigation has revealed spending on agency social workers has gone up by nearly a third in the last year. Unison professional officer Helga Pile said the agency spend was "a really unhealthy situation".
>
> It does seem some are making the decision to go over to agency work to get some control back in terms of pressures in their departments. (Community Care, 2015)

One way of comparing agency rates of SWs with other similar professions such as teachers and nurses is by analysing data from the Labour Force Survey (LFS). The LFS is the largest regular social survey which collects information on the UK labour market and is therefore of use when analysing trends in respect of labour market issues. The LFS is a longitudinal survey: a series of measurements taken over time. I looked in depth at the LFS data for 2017 and found that SWs were significantly more likely to be agency workers than teachers (by ten times), nurses and other occupations which engage agency staff. While there may be different reasons for SWs to decide to work for an agency, one obvious hypothesis is that they get paid significantly more for agency work, which in turn allows them to take more time off. As the Unison Officer quoted earlier suggests, the increasing numbers of SWs turning to agency work could be because SWs want to get more control back in terms of the pressures exerted upon them and have more freedom to move roles regularly.

The impact of managerialism

The Munro Review of Child Protection (2012) argued that SWs need to assert their professional standing and develop their expertise in working with families. It ventured that this would subsequently lead to a move away from the compliance and blame culture within child protection services, and towards a learning culture in which professional judgement and effective relationships with service users enable the improvement of services to vulnerable children and families.

Despite the findings of the Munro review, in many LAs the persistent impact of managerialism has meant that the task of understanding what a child's life is like and then working alongside parents and children to deliver appropriate and effective support has proven increasingly difficult (Diaz and Drewery, 2016). This is largely attributable to the constraints that the bureaucratic system places on SWs (Burgess et al, 2013). Concerns remain that SWs are under pressure from SMs to reach targets based largely on timescales and not on the quality of the work (Diaz and Drewery, 2016). Accordingly, management can be overly concerned with 'doing things in the right way rather than doing the right thing' (Munro, 2011, p 6).

For Howe (2006), the decline in the status of social work has coincided with an increase in external controls from managers, LAs (who employ most SWs) and the central government. As SWs are increasingly more likely to be under the control of bureaucrats and managers, arguably this will lead to their professional knowledge being devalued (Fabricant and Burghardt, 1992). Targets and quantitative data thus become the priority, rather than the undertaking of high-quality work to improve the life opportunities of children and their families (Diaz and Drewery, 2016).

Munro (2012) contends that as a result of reforms and the modernisation agenda, SWs have become overly focused on completing assessments within arbitrary timescales. Hood et al (2016) also assert that despite the Munro review (2012), LAs are still largely focused on compliance and performance management and that this is in part due to the impact of the Ofsted inspections. They conclude that 'the paucity of outcome measures but also of evidence-based process measures have reinforced a dependence on procedural compliance backed up by a centralised inspectorate' (Hood et al, 2016, p 930).

Outcomes for children

Outcomes for children who have been in LA care have been widely researched and plotted. This group consistently have some of the worst outcomes of all children (DfE, 2016). Almost one third of children in care leave school with no qualifications (The Who Cares? Trust, 2016). A quarter of young women leaving care are pregnant or are already mothers, and a high proportion of the babies born to mothers who are or who have been in care are removed into care themselves (Roberts et al, 2017). Children in care are five times more likely to suffer from mental illness than children nationally (The Centre for Social Justice, 2007), and 40 per cent of prisoners under 21 years of age have been in care.

Children who come into care are likely to have been maltreated at home (Wade et al, 2011). They subsequently face further discrimination as a result of being in care, and eventually having left care (Barnes, 2012). While being placed in care will not be able to undo past mistreatment, one expectation on LAs should be that children who leave care are better equipped for adulthood than they otherwise would have been.

This gloomy picture, however, does not tell the whole story. Comparing outcomes for children who have been in care against those who have had involvement with social work services but stayed at home is challenging. It is difficult to disentangle whether their outcomes are a product of care system failings, the effect of abuse, multiple returns to an abusive home (Forrester et al, 2009) or a combination of all three. Recent research (Wade et al, 2011) suggests that pre-care adversities are particularly influential and are likely to impact on children's outcomes and life chances. Forrester's (2008) research suggests that children's welfare does improve while they are in care. Similarly, Ofsted comments in its 2017 Annual Report that 'care can be good for children' and that children see their life chances improved from where they otherwise would have been had they remained at home (Ofsted, 2017).

Many care-experienced people do go on to become successful adults. Moreover, the outcomes for children in care are better overall than those for children who are the subjects of LA Children's Services on a long-term basis as 'children in need' and never enter the care system (Sebba et al, 2015; Berridge et al, 2015). Wade et al (2011) found that contrary to common beliefs, long-term care can be a positive option for maltreated children. Similarly, a large-scale study by Selwyn and Briheim-Crookall (2017) concluded that 83 per cent of children in care said that coming into care had improved their well-being. In summary, care can be a very positive experience for many young people, and indeed, it is often necessary as it is not safe for them to remain living at home with their parents.

Structure of the book

In Chapter 2, I consider current thinking on children's and parents' participation in decision making. Drawing on a range of academic papers and reports, I consider what participation means, exploring theoretical concepts such as Hart's (1992) 'ladder' of participation. A critical analysis of current legislation and policy in the UK relating to child-centred practice and parental and children's participation will follow.

I then go on to consider parents' and children's views of the child protection system and, in particular, Child Protection Conferences and Child protection SWs. Chapter 3 is based on interviews with 40 children and 52 parents in two LAs whose children were subject to a Child Protection Plan at the time. The field study found that most parents felt unsupported throughout the child protection process, reporting feelings of powerlessness, intimidation and fear. Parents reported that they found Child Protection Conferences particularly stigmatising and oppressive and this led to them not trusting SWs and other key agencies. The majority stated that they did not find their SWs to be helpful, a reality which could increase the likelihood of disengagement and inhibit change. Some parents said that they felt sorry for their SWs and considered that they seemed stressed, clearly under too much pressure and often did not do what they said they would do. It was interesting to note how aware parents were of SW's high caseloads and the bureaucratic pressures they faced.

This chapter also considers children's and young people's views of the child protection system and their SWs, as well as their knowledge and awareness of Child Protection Plans. It considers young people's views on the extent to which SWs have helped improve their lives and what they consider to be the barriers to and enablers of good child protection practice. This chapter highlights the high number of SWs young participants had, as well as exploring their relationships with their SW and their perception of the Child Protection Conference.

Chapter 4 considers children's views of the care system and CiC reviews. This chapter details the views of 35 young people in care about their experiences of SWs, IROs and the care system and the extent to which they felt their voice was being heard both in review meetings and in day-to-day practice. Young participants reported finding CiC reviews frustrating and stressful, often due in part to poor relationships with SWs. They also conveyed scepticism about the value of the review process. The chapter highlights the importance of the role of IROs, who generally stay in their roles longer than SWs and can therefore provide more consistent relationships with young people in care. Young people discussed how at times they were not invited to meetings as the SWs' and IROs' priority was ensuring the meeting took place within a certain timescale. Overall, young people reported that they did not feel that CiC reviews enabled them to meaningfully participate. One ray of light is the developing practice of children chairing their own reviews; the chapter ends with a call for this to be developed alongside other creative methods of allowing young people to play a meaningful part in meetings that affect them.

In Chapter 5, I consider SWs' and IROs' views of children's participation, specifically in the context of the work they carry out with children in care. Pressures on professionals were a recurrent concern. It was also noted that SWs' understanding of the concept of participation was limited and the examples provided illustrated that children's and young people's participation was largely tokenistic. There appeared to be a disconnect/dissonance between professionals' views of how important participation is and their actual practice with families. While both SWs and IROs stated that children's participation was very important to them, it was telling that they then went on to explain that generally children played no role in deciding key logistical factors in respect of the review meeting itself. SWs and IROs also stated that reviews took place without children present so as to meet statutory timescales and that, on occasion, CiC reviews would immediately follow Personal Education Plan (PEP) meetings, thus leading to very lengthy meetings. Despite legislation giving children the right to have a say about their care and for their wishes to be taken into consideration, there remains a lack of commitment to this from professionals. High caseloads, systemic pressures and a focus on completing paperwork rather than engaging meaningfully with children seem to be at the heart of this. This resonates with Forrester's (2016) concept of 'zombie social work', and appears to be clear evidence of 'doing things right instead of doing the right thing' (Munro, 2012).

Chapter 6 outlines SMs' views of children's participation. This chapter considers the views of SMs, which are presented alongside a discussion of the rise in managerialism in social work. There was an observable contrast between the views of SMs and the perspectives of the other participants interviewed for this study, particularly in relation to workload challenges faced by SWs and IROs. SMs appeared to blame individual SWs when things went wrong, and despite some SWs in the field site LA having caseloads of up to 40 children, SMs did not seem to see this as an issue. SMs also displayed limited understanding of 'meaningful participation', and were unsure of the opportunities children had to participate or how they could support this. They reported that little seemed to have changed with children's participation in their reviews over the last 25 years. It was striking to note that young people seemed to have a better understanding of the pressures faced by SWs than SMs.

In Chapter 7, I consider children's and professionals' views of complaints. This chapter looks at the complaints process which is followed when children in care wish to express dissatisfaction with the services they receive. Despite the introduction of guidelines and procedures aimed at encouraging and supporting children and young people to complain about the services they receive, children in care still face barriers to doing so in practice. Following semi-structured interviews with children in care, SWs, SMs and IROs from two English LAs, the research uncovered a number of issues of concern. Complaints by children in care were found to be managed at the lowest possible level, and SMs demonstrated an overly optimistic view about children in care being informed of complaint procedures and being encouraged to engage with them. Children in care were found to be worried about complaining, the consequence being that their voices are often not heard. However, when issues were clearly defined, IROs had some degree of success in resolving their complaints.

Chapter 8 provides a summary of the key research findings from this study, along with my concluding thoughts. I outline the study's key messages as well as recommendations for policy and practice. This chapter highlights the changes that need to take place, not just systemically but also in terms of practice by individual IROs and SWs. In particular, it outlines how the caseloads of SWs need to be reduced in order to allow SW to support families properly.

2

Children's and parents' participation: current thinking

Lorna Stabler

Introduction

This chapter seeks to ground the reader in some of the key concepts and thinking relevant to the research that populates the following chapters. It starts by considering what participation means, and for whom, exploring theoretical concepts such as Arnstein's ladder of participation (1969) and Hart's (1992) later adaption for the context of children's participation, as well as other frameworks particularly useful for exploring participation in public services.

This is followed by an exploration of some of the key issues and considerations specific to participation in the context of children's social care. How participation is defined tends to differ depending on who is 'participating', in what context and for what end. In this chapter, we are particularly interested in participation within children's social care, meaning the two groups that we will be exploring when discussing participation will be children and young people and parents within children's social care.

The rest of the chapter is then given to exploring some of the research relevant to the involvement of parents and children in social care decision making – namely through meetings held with professionals. In particular, this section focuses on the roles of professionals in enabling meaningful participation in decision making, and some of the challenges involved.

What is participation?

Participation is an important concept in many sectors, from international development to information services to product design. Consequently, reaching a definition of participation is complicated by the terminology differing across disciplines, with a vast array of language to describe 'best practice'. This can mean that the literature can be daunting to begin with. Participation is often used interchangeably with words such as 'consultation', 'partnership' or 'involvement' (Croft and Beresford, 1992; Roberts, 2002).

Types of participation can be divided into two categories: individual participation and collective participation (Kennan et al, 2016). Some disciplines are concerned with both types, but many western interpretations focus more on individual participation than on collective participation. With regard to service delivery, this is arguably driven by the consumerist notion of a citizen, whereby a service (be it public or profit driven) is delivered to meet the needs and requirements of a rational individual, who presumably could take their business elsewhere if the service was deficit in any way.

This notion presents problems for public (social) services, where there is a limited (if any) element of choice for service users. This is even more problematic where services (such as child protection or justice) may be delivered against the will of the individual.

This shows it is not possible to develop a 'catch all' definition of participation. It is necessary to consider what is meant by participation within the context that it is being applied. For adult service users then, the concept of participation is often closely linked with that of coproduction, in that it is important for service users to be involved not just in choosing to 'take part' (as this is often not a real choice) but in making key decisions and shaping what services look like and how they are managed and delivered.

Within social services, often participation is discussed as 'service user involvement', referring to a social policy development of modernisation of public services since the 1990s (Warren and Cook, 2005). As Smith et al (2011) describe, service user involvement has been drawn on to address everything from strengthening communities, increasing citizenship and promoting social inclusion; improving the design and delivery of services and ensuring that services better meet the needs of those who use them; and empowering service users, students and educators.

Two key components of participation seem clear:

- It is a process and not a one-off event (Larkins et al, 2014; Fylkesnes et al, 2018).
- It enables the person to have an influence on their outcomes (Kennan et al, 2016; McDowall, 2016).

This is consistent with the UNCRC definition of participation as being 'widely used to describe ongoing processes, which include information-sharing and dialogue between children and adults based on mutual respect, and in which children can learn how their views and those of adults are taken into account and shape the outcome of such processes'.

Why is participation important?

For citizens in modern democracies, the concept of participation is central to that of the democratic system and is necessary for the political and social structures that exist. But participation is not uncontroversial. Critiques have emerged in numerous disciplines where the participatory approach has been embraced. The main critique is that it can be expensive and time consuming to do well, and even then may not have the transformative power that was hoped.

However, in sectors where power dynamics are built into structures, and the consequences of decisions can be life changing, the concept of participation seems, at least in principle, an obvious necessity.

Within public services, Foot et al (2014) summarise six perspectives from which service user participation can be viewed:

1. A consumerist approach: health and social care are seen as a marketplace in which service users (consumers) are involved by making choices about services, and the health care market responds to their preferences. User involvement is then a means to improve quality.
2. A democratic approach: people have political, social and economic rights as citizens, and those who use or are affected by a public service should be involved in how it is run and have certain rights regarding what they receive from that service.
3. An ethical and outcomes-based approach: involvement is seen as the ethical thing to do, and the best approach to improve outcomes. This means recognising that good care comprises the application to individual circumstances of evidence-based care and service provision along with knowledge and experience. User involvement is essential to the judgement of relative risk and benefit associated with decision making.
4. A value-based approach: to achieve truly the best value for money, a health and care system must know and respond to what people need and want. In this way, care can meet needs and preferences.
5. A sustainability-based approach: by involving people in managing their own health and care, and keeping well and independent, use

of statutory services can be minimised and community resources can be harnessed.

6. A person-centred care approach: health and care systems should focus on their users, promoting independence and be co-ordinated around people's full needs rather than being fragmented and siloed. Service-user involvement is an essential component of delivering a more person-centred service that is tailored and responsive to individual needs and values.

For children, the rationale is similar, but with a different emphasis. Dickens et al (2015) highlighted five perspectives which consider the rationale for children's participation:

1. promote development and self-confidence;
2. improve the decisions being made and the practice of the agency;
3. enable child's voice to be heard and therefore contribute to safeguarding them from what is happening in their lives;
4. consider children as active social beings who should be able to take part in decision making;
5. understand that involvement is key to children's rights.

Each of these perspectives highlights the many elements of practice that participation hopes to impact, showing the arguably broad remit of participation. Participation is not designed as an end in itself; rather, it is a process which, if effective, can be beneficial to the recipient (Malone and Hartung, 2010). Conversely, mismanagement of the process could prove distressing or even harmful (Cossar et al, 2011).

The promise of participation indicates a need for clear objectives for anyone who believes in a participatory approach and wants it to have the impact that it promises.

Theoretical concepts of participation

While the practice of participation arguably does not need a set framework, the theorising of participation has led to countless models being developed. Participation is a multifaceted concept (McDowall, 2016) and has been described as 'messy, fluid and relational' (Larkins et al, 2014). The definition of participation is contested and can be defined in different ways (Križ and Skivenes, 2017). Moreover, practices of participation are different for adults and children, have various challenges and are interpreted differently in legislation and practice.

Citizen participation

The concept of participation is widely associated with democracy and the relationship between the state (those holding the power) and the rest of the population (the citizens). This relationship is a key tenet of democratic legitimacy. However, the way in which this participation actually works in practice has received an increasing amount of academic interest.

Arnstein's ladder of participation

One of the main starting points when theorising citizen participation is Sherry Arnstein's work. Writing in 1969 about citizen involvement in planning processes in the United States, Arnstein described a 'ladder of citizen participation' that showed degrees of participation ranging from high to low.

The ladder is a guide to seeing who has power when important decisions are being made. The ladder makes the distinction between tokenism or non-participation and 'partnership' in which citizens have an equal voice to those in power. The rungs can be described as levels of participation:

Figure 2.1: Degrees of participation

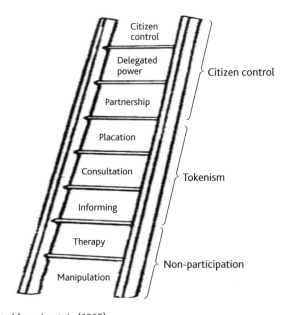

Source: Adapted from Arnstein (1969)

Non-participation

1. Manipulation and 2. Therapy: The aim is to cure or educate the participants. The proposed plan is the best and any participation pursued is to achieve public support through public relations rather than change or influence what has been already decided.

Tokenism

3. Informing: An important first step to legitimate participation but frequently the emphasis is on a one-way flow of information without a channel for feedback.
4. Consultation: Again a legitimate step which includes ways of gaining opinions (such as attitude surveys, neighbourhood meetings and public enquiries). However, Arnstein argued that this is more 'window dressing' than power sharing.
5. Placation: For example, co-option of hand-picked representatives onto committees who are likely to agree with the status quo. It allows citizens to advise or plan ad infinitum but retains for power holders the right to judge the legitimacy or feasibility of the advice.

Citizen control

6. Partnership: Power is redistributed through negotiation between citizens and power holders. Planning and decision-making responsibilities are shared, for example, through joint committees.
7. Delegation: Citizens hold a clear majority of seats on committees with delegated powers to make decisions. The public has the power to assure accountability of the programme to them.
8 Citizen Control: Citizens rather than those in power handle the entire job of planning, policy making and managing a programme, for example, neighbourhood corporation with no intermediaries between it and the source of funds.

Hart's ladder of participation

Hart (1992) built on Arnstein's model to consider children's participation. He argued that the growth of children's rights had led to an increasing recognition of children's abilities to speak for themselves but that this had not translated into meaningful participation of children in decision making.

Figure 2.2: Hart's ladder of participation

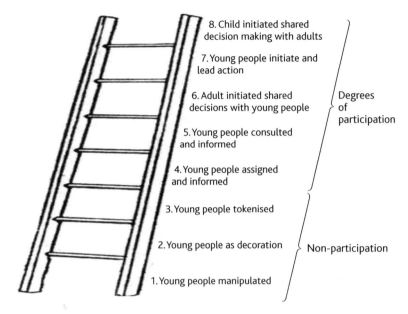

Source: Adapted from UNICEF Innocenti Research Centre

In response, his ladder of children's participation sought to show the role that children could play as citizens. Commonly used as a tool to evaluate participatory processes, the ladder provides a description of various 'levels' of participation, ranging from manipulation to partnership working, in which children have an equal voice to adults (Bessell and Gal, 2009). This pertains to the empowering effect of participation for children and the link between participation, self-esteem and confidence (Cashmore, 2002).

Hart (1992) acknowledges that the level of participation will differ depending upon the context and child involved. However, non-participation of children and young people (rungs 1, 2 and 3), particularly using them to project an image of participation without allowing them any real influence, can be damaging for children.

The evolution of frameworks for children's participation

Theoretical conceptions have considered the way in which participation of children needs to work as 'building blocks' towards 'full' participation. Rather than full citizen participation at the outset, there may be a need to work with children and young people to get them to the point of sharing decision making. For example, depending on age, development and/or understanding, some children may not be able to begin on the top rungs of Hart's model but require support to develop the skills and understanding needed to reach a place where they are able to initiate and share decision making. Within this, there are other factors to consider, such as the role of other people and structures to enable and ensure children's participation.

Addressing this, Harry Shier (2001) focused on the need for organisations and adults to be committed to children's participation in order for it to be realistic. His Pathways to Participation identified five levels of participation, with questions for organisations to consider whether they are ready and committed to children's participation. In reflecting on these questions, organisations could ensure that what they were doing to involve children was not tokenistic and could fit within other organisational processes.

Other models, such as Thomas' (2002) 'Climbing Wall of participation', highlighted the role of other factors in ensuring children's participation, such as the support available to children to be able to participate or the range and legitimacy of opportunities provided to them to participate. All these models of children's participation highlight that it is a staged and complex process that needs both the education and development of the child and also the adaption of organisations and evolution of adult mindsets to be meaningful and worthwhile for the service and for the child.

Rights and needs

There are other concepts that are important to take into account when developing an understanding of participation. In particular, participation has been discussed as fundamental to upholding human rights and also as an important human need.

Participation as a right

Central to the rights-based perspective of participation is that the state is accountable to citizens as bearers of rights and that basic principles of democracy holds that all citizens have a right to participate (either directly or indirectly through representatives of their own choosing) in decisions that critically affect their personal interests. A core element of this is that citizens therefore must know their rights and be able to challenge the state (or service providers) who do not uphold these rights. For participation to be truly rights based, services need to

Figure 2.3: Pathways to participation: openings, opportunities and obligations

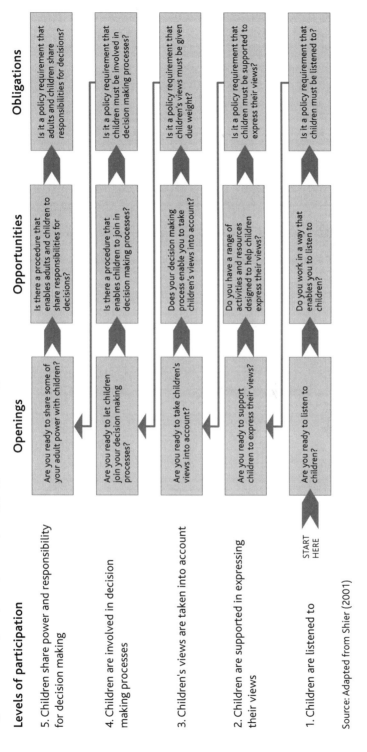

Source: Adapted from Shier (2001)

include stakeholders in every facet of the service delivery process, ensuring they understand and have the capacity to make decisions.

Theories drawn from a 'rights' basis with regard to children refer more broadly to the participation of children within society. The Children's Rights Charter (CRC) is the most accepted and common source for defining children's participation (Leviner, 2018). Based on the CRC, two aspects of children's right to participation are commonly emphasised (Melton, 2005). First, participation is an overall principle in the CRC, which refers to a set of rights and freedoms: freedom of expression (article 13), freedom of thought, conscience and religion (article 14), freedom of association and peaceful assembly (article 15), the right to privacy (article 16) and access to mass media (article 17). Second, children's right to participation is also an independent right, as expressed in article 12 of the CRC, which states that every child who is capable of forming his or her own views should have the right to express those views freely in all matters affecting them and those views should be given due weight in accordance with the child's age and maturity.

Within a child's rights approach to participation, care and protection from harm is re-characterised as entitlement, rather than an act of adult benevolence (Bessell and Gal, 2009). This has consequences for the nature of participation with children, who are depicted as 'citizens' irrespective of age and capacity, with rights, as a member of society. This approach lends itself to viewing children as resources with something to offer society (Bessell and Gal, 2009), essentially as 'experts' on childhood (Hale, 2006). However, this perspective is not without limitations. The suggestion is that a rights rhetoric can lend itself to viewing those who do require protection and social provision as dependents who lack competency (Minow, 1990). This highlights the tension between legislation and theory in the context of child protection social work (Lansdown, 2010). Children must be heard (legally and in guidance) but must also be protected from adult issues – raising questions of how possible 'partnership' is and what level of participation can and should be realistically aimed for in the child protection context.

Participation as a need

An alternative stance for understanding and justifying child participation is supported by theories of child development (Bessell and Gal, 2009) in which participation in decision making is characterised as a basic need akin to health and autonomy. In their discussion of participation as a need, Bessell and Gal (2009) draw on a number of studies with children and young people to justify this stance. However, links appear, at times, tenuous between the aims of the studies they draw upon and their view of a basic need, which is never actually defined. Nonetheless, the discussion of children's needs in the context of participation is useful, particularly in terms of the positive effect of participation and the moral argument for involving children in decisions about their care put forward by the UNCRC (1989).

Inextricably linked to this are the by-products of participation and feeling heard, which are building confidence and self-esteem; these are invaluable when preparing children and young people for independence (Bostock, 2005). Cashmore (2002) reviewed the research literature from the UK, North America, Australia and New Zealand in relation to the perceptions of children and young people in care about the extent to which they have been able to participate in decisions that affect them. Involvement in the decision–making process was shown to result in a greater sense of satisfaction with the outcome of any decision made, whether desired or not (Cashmore, 2002).

Participation within children's social care

Within a children's social care context, the definition can be further complicated by the balancing of participation and 'protection' of children, and the perception of potentially competing rights of parents and children. This can be an acute issue for SWs in circumstances where children may have experienced harm within their families. McLaughlin (2009, p 1593) captures the problem thus:

> [T]here is a point in social work practice whereby the social worker is expected to act on their own professional assessment of the situation, informed by agency policy, legal mandates and research, irrespective of what the service user's choices or views are.

Despite this complexity, partnership with families has a long history in services for children and families, and partnership principles underpin the Children Act 1989, related policies and procedures and much subsequent legislation (DoH, 1989). Moreover, the right for children, young people and families to be involved in decision making about their lives, and for plans to be focused on their individual needs, is well argued in social work literature and practice (Merkel-Holguin et al, 2019).

Notably, since 2000 in the UK has seen an acknowledgement of the rights of children, young people and parents to participate in developing services both for them individually and for the wider community. LA and partner agencies have begun to acknowledge that, when listened to, children, young people and parents can play an essential role in the planning and delivery of services (Miller and McNicholl, 2003; DfE, 2014).

As a result of the changes outlined, participation has become a key 'target' in many voluntary and statutory organisations that work with vulnerable children and families. At times, this can lead to the 'participation "box" being ticked by organisations because they can demonstrate that they have involved children and young people in a specific activity, rather than because they can provide evidence of change or improvement as a result of their participation' (SCIE, 2012).

Wilkins (2013) suggests that all work with children and families should involve service users in planning and review and that professionals should put themselves into the shoes of the service user and implement the core social work values of choice, independence and personal welfare to work alongside families to improve their life opportunities. It is therefore important to consider how effectively SWs and other professionals work in partnership with children and parents when there are concerns that the children are at risk of abuse or neglect, and specifically when children come into care. One of the key principles of the Children Act 1989 is the importance of working in partnership with parents. Between 50 and 70 per cent of children who come into care end up returning to live with their parents (Farmer, 2014). Therefore, it is essential that SWs have meaningful and, as far as possible, positive working relationships with both parents and children.

The extent to which this happens in practice is negotiable. Križ and Skivenes (2017) found that workers often mistake consultation for participation, with 40 per cent of English and 35 per cent of US workers interviewed embracing views of children's participation that can be considered token or non-participation. Havlicek et al (2018) also found discrepancies between workers' conceptualisations of youth participation and the strategies they enact within programmes. This could be due in part to the ambiguity around the terminology. With regard to children's participation, the terms participation, involvement and consultation have been found to be used on an interchangeable basis. Useful definitions are:

- **Consultation:** gathering children's or young people's views on a particular issue or question;

- **Participation:** children and young people joining in the decision making;
- **Involvement:** where adults give children and young people opportunities and support to take part.

These inter-related definitions show further the complex nature of what, taken at face value, seems an inarguable concept and also highlight the need for training for those working with families and children in order to develop a shared understanding of what participation is.

Participation by children and young people in children's social care

In considering the importance of participation for children in care, the UNCRC (1989) is a useful starting point. All countries except the United States and Somalia have ratified this treaty. Children's rights include their right to association with both parents; human identity; basic needs for physical protection and food; universal state-paid education; health care; criminal laws appropriate for the age and development of the child; equal protection of the child's civil rights; and freedom from discrimination on the basis of the child's race, gender, sexual orientation, gender identity, national origin, religion, disability, colour, ethnicity, or other characteristics (UNCRC, 1989).

In 2013, the DfE announced a policy commitment to improving outcomes for young people. A significant part of this is ensuring that young people have opportunities to participate in decisions that affect them (DfE, 2013a). However, although there have been positive steps forward in young people's involvement:

> The key issue is not participation or no participation, but whether adults are genuinely attentive and responsive to young people's perspectives, and aware of the plurality and polyphony of their voices. (Hartas and Lindsay, 2011, p 131)

For example, McLeod (2006) carried out qualitative interviews with SWs and young people in care to explore the effectiveness of communication between them. SWs indicated that they had made extensive efforts to listen to children and promote participation. However, young people reported that they felt their views had not been heard or taken into account when decisions were made. This disparity raises questions regarding how best to support children and young people to engage in meaningful participation, rather than what could be viewed as tokenistic and having little impact on the decisions made.

The extent to which a child's or young person's views are taken into consideration is the result of a wide range of factors, which is reflected in empirical research with social work professionals. For example, Shemmings (2000) asked 88 professionals working in family and child protection services (42 SWs and 46 non-SWs) to complete a questionnaire aimed at finding out their views about (i) the age at which children should make certain decisions and (ii) whether children should be involved in Child Protection Conferences. This was followed up with qualitative data whereby detailed notes were made when 25 of the SWs discussed their views during a training day exercise. The study concluded that the professionals valued the desire to 'protect' children from harm, including from what could be deemed as 'adult' decisions, more than the desire to uphold children's right to participate.

Furthermore, children and young people may make choices not to participate, either as a genuine choice or as a means to abdicate responsibility, although where this fits into the ladder is unclear (Cashmore, 2002). Vis et al (2010) undertook a study in Norway with 53 child protection case managers and 33 social work students. Participants completed a questionnaire in which they were asked to agree or disagree with 20 statements about child participation. The research concluded that the views of professionals were a key barrier to the participation of children in children's social work. While the relevance of this study to the UK system is somewhat limited as it was completed in Norway, and Norwegian social work professionals will have been trained in a different manner to those in the UK, the study does support the theory that professionals' understanding of participation is indicative of a system in which 'adults within or associated with the system tend to act as gatekeepers, determining when, if and how children's views might be treated seriously' (Bessell and Gal, 2009, p 287).

With regard to children in care, arguments for the importance of participation focus upon the very nature of being 'in care'. Children who have been accommodated by the LA have often been removed from their parents' care in distressing circumstances and may have experienced neglectful parenting and instability of care arrangements (Wade et al, 2011).

They enter a world in which the number and type of decisions made are very different to those children who are not in the care system, and they have a disproportionate level of contact with professionals. For children in care, there are regular and numerous decisions to be made in relation to their education, health and well-being. There are a variety of different people who will play a role in this decision making, including SWs and foster carers. At times, decisions are made in relation to children in care by professionals who have never even met the young person (Thomas and O'Kane, 1999). Empowering children in care to participate in these decisions is particularly important in ensuring that the child's needs are properly understood and met.

Despite changes to guidance within the care system (Thoburn, 2010), children and young people in care have reported that they feel they have limited opportunities to engage in decisions about their lives (Thomas and O'Kane, 1999; Munro, 2001; Cashmore, 2002; Pert et al, 2014). The views of children in care have been gained in a variety of guises over the last decade: through involvement in decision-making processes (Hallett, 2000), the efficacy of children's advocates (Barnes, 2012), the role of IROs (Ofsted, 2013a; Pert et al, 2014; Dickens et al, 2015), care planning and the courts (Timms and Thoburn, 2006) and, more broadly, experiences of the care system (Ofsted, 2011a, 2011b). Overall, these studies suggest that children and young people tend to have an ineffective voice and limited power in review meetings and that they are not actively involved in the decision-making processes. Sadly, these findings remain apparent nearly 30 years after the right for children to participate in decisions made about them was enshrined in the Children Act 1989, raising concerns regarding professionals' ability to properly ensure that young people participate in decision making which affects them. Indeed, the UNCRC itself has commented that the UK in its implementation of article 12 'seemed to suggest that consulting the child on his or her view was a matter of discretion rather than a right' (cited in Murray and Hallett, 2000, p 15).

Participation in decision-making forums

In the context of childcare social work, two of the formal mechanisms in which decisions about children are made are Child Protection Conferences and CiC reviews. A Child Protection Conference is a multi-agency meeting that aims to ensure children's safety, promote children's health and development and identify when a child is at risk of significant harm. About 20 per cent of children who are made subject to a Child Protection Plan end up coming into care (DfE, 2015). In a similar way to CiC reviews, law and policies in the UK highlight the importance of children and parents being involved in Child Protection Conferences and their wishes and feelings being heard by professionals (DfE, 2015).

Yet there is a substantial body of evidence indicating that, despite children's social care meetings with professionals and families being a key forum for making decisions (Healy and Darlington, 2009), many meetings such as child protection case conferences do not seem to embody or enable principles of self-determination for parents and children. Perhaps because of this, they are often reported to be very difficult for parents and, when they attend, children (see, for instance, Corby et al, 1996; Bell, 1999; Hall and Slembrouck, 2001). As these are the key points at which decisions are made, and potentially the only opportunity that families have available to them to input formally into decision making, it is important that meaningful participation is built into how these meetings take place.

Family group conferencing

In response to concerns such as these, there have been attempts to reform existing meetings and the development of new types of meetings to involve families with an emphasis on the realisation of their rights. In particular, a body of research emphasises the political and social principles that services such as family group conferencing can enable (Ashley and Nixon, 2007; Edwards and Parkinson, 2018). Similar approaches, such as Family Team Decision Making, Family Involvement Meetings and case planning have been introduced in many different contexts globally (Thørnblad et al, 2016).

Most of these approaches stem from family group conferencing. A family group conference is a way of transforming decision making and planning for children into a process led by family members (like the 'citizen control' element of Arnstein's ladder). Children and young people can also be directly involved in their family group conference, usually with the support of an advocate.

Family group conferences draw upon Maori culture, and their development was a response to the large number of Maori children being removed into state institutions. Family group conferences are now recognised in law in New Zealand as being the key process by which families make informed and responsible decisions, recommendations and plans for their children and young people. Family group conferences have been adapted and used in different contexts across the world and are used in a large number of countries at decision-making points.

These approaches have in common an attempt to redesign meetings in a way that can enable the involvement of family and the wider community in important decisions. Some of these (although by no means all) are specifically focused on children at high risk of care or who may be reunified with their families after a period of time in care. These meetings aim to involve the family network in decision making and planning about the safety and care of a child, with the objective of reducing the reliance on out–of–home care and child removal from the family network (Marsh and Crow, 1998).

There is some research which theorises that meetings that are designed to include families in decision making might reduce the need for children to be in care in a number of ways. For example, it has been argued that if families can be engaged in meetings that emphasise family participation in decision making, families may be likely to engage with SWs in a meaningful way (Muench et al, 2017). In turn, including parents in planning could be a motivating force for parents to work alongside professionals to make agreed plans work, increasing the likelihood of change (Faller, 1981; Featherstone et al, 2018).

Moreover, by engaging with a wider family network, and including them in planning, it is possible that the resources available to the family can be harnessed to ensure that the child can remain safely in the home (Appleton, 2015). This could be due to making more people aware of the difficulties that the family is facing and therefore allowing them the opportunity to offer support (Morris et al, 2007) or through getting a clearer understanding of the situation of the family (Marsh and Crow, 1998). This could help to ensure children are safe through partnership working with families to identify and strengthen the safety net for children at risk of harm (Morris et al, 2007).

Importantly, these meetings have been proposed as a way to reduce the disproportionate representation of children from ethnic minority backgrounds in the children's social care system (Nygård and Saus, 2019). This is particularly relevant in the US, Australian and New Zealand contexts, but could apply in the UK also.

Children's participation in social care decision making

Article 12 of the UNCRC (1989) most clearly sets out the right of children to participate in decisions which are about or affect them (Cashmore, 2002). The UK, as a signatory, is therefore expected to uphold the child's right to express their views and have them taken into account. Notably, this does not necessitate the right to make decisions or be part of the decision–making process (Schofield and Thoburn, 1996). Rather, the focus is upon being listened to, with the views of the child respected and given due consideration (Cashmore, 2002).

A recent study carried out on behalf of the Children's Commissioner for England has considered children's views of Child Protection Conferences (Cossar et al, 2011). This research was conducted in collaboration with one LA in London. As this study was carried out in just one LA, it is important to recognise that it cannot claim external validity. Children and young people aged between 5 and 18 who had been subject to a Child Protection Plan in the previous 12 months and who were not currently in public care were identified. Eighteen families agreed to take part, providing a sample of 26 children in total. Children and young people were involved throughout the research process. Young people on the research advisory group provided insights at the design, data collection and analysis stages of the research and helped to write a young person's version of the report. Findings indicated that only a small minority of children were aware of different ways in which their views could be provided at the meeting. Most of the children who attended conferences found them difficult and few felt even partly listened to. The authors highlighted the potential harm caused from participation where children are not adequately prepared or offered choice in how to participate.

A similar conclusion was also drawn by van Bijleveld et al (2013). In this study, the authors carried out a comprehensive review of the literature available on child participation within child welfare and child protection. They used keyword searches to identify relevant papers and augmented the search with literature included in article reference lists. They identified 21 studies of relevance dating from 1995 to 2012. They consistently found that children would say that they should always participate, whereas SWs outlined many situations where, in their view, children's participation is inappropriate. Muench et al (2017) interviewed 23 children and 26 corresponding parents, all of whom were going through the child protection process. This study was carried out in just one LA so it cannot claim external validity but can provide us with useful insights into service users' views. The study suggested that children and young people felt inadequately involved throughout the child protection process and were not able to make informed choices.

While there has been some recent research into the views of children within the child protection arena (Cossar et al, 2011; Muench et al, 2017), with regard to children in care reviews both historical and recent empirical research aimed at gaining the views of children is sparse

(Thomas, 2011). The largest study to consider the participation of children in care in their review meetings was by Thomas and O'Kane (1999). The study carried out a quantitative survey of 225 children aged 8 to 12 years in seven LA areas. This was followed up with a qualitative study of 47 cases where they interviewed the children, their SWs, carers and some of the parents. They also held focus groups with young people and observed a small number of meetings. The authors concluded that only half of the children interviewed attended their review meetings, and those who did largely found them 'boring' or 'scary'. Furthermore, over a third reported having very little influence within the meeting. However, it should be noted that the participants were identified by SWs rather than the researcher, potentially affecting the validity of the findings.

The participation of children in their reviews (based on understanding the purpose and content of them) has been questioned (Munro, 2001), and exploration of preparation and choice in how and when reviews are held has also been highlighted as limited (Sinclair, 1998). Unsurprisingly then, conclusions have been drawn that young people feel disillusioned with the review process and that their views are not listened to (Thomas, 2011). A common theme in the research is that 'most [children] report that the purpose of the meeting is to talk about, rather than to, them' (Munro, 2001, p 135). Indeed, both Munro (2001) and Sinclair (1998) called for reconsideration as to whether the review meeting itself was an appropriate vehicle to promote participation. Other research has identified that consulting children and young people was not enough to ensure their views had an impact on the decisions which were made at their review meetings (Vis et al, 2010). This raises questions regarding how meaningful participation is achieved by practitioners.

The number of children attending review meetings is consistently low. The DfE (2016) has published national statistics regarding the attendance of children in their reviews and the means by which they participated. The statistics relate to children aged four or over who had been looked after by the LA for four weeks or more. The data evidence that in 2007, 48 per cent of children physically attended their reviews and spoke for themselves; this dropped to 46 per cent in 2009 and 43 per cent in 2011 but increased to 44 per cent in 2014. The percentage of children who did not attend but who conveyed their views by a facilitated medium was 11 per cent in 2007, increasing to 12 per cent in 2010 and 14 per cent in 2014 (DfE, 2016). These figures indicate that despite the increasing profile of the importance of participation, participation rates have not significantly increased. It is also somewhat surprising that despite the myriad of different forms of technology available, the number of children who conveyed their views by a facilitated medium has remained stubbornly low.

As a way of addressing children's involvement in decision making, there has been an emphasis on ensuring that meetings are held in a manner that highlights their role, rather than include them in a tokenistic way. A recent review (Stabler et al, 2019) looked at what mechanisms are important when including children and young people in social care meeting in order to enable them to be meaningfully involved in an often-adult-orientated forum. In this, three key mechanisms were identified:

- **Collaboration and engagement**: *before the meeting* working with the child/young person so that they are fully prepared for what the meeting is about, what it will look like, what might be shared; *during the meeting* the child/young person has access to an advocate to support them to take part; *after the meeting* the child/young person is offered support that is relevant to their preferences and needs based on people at the meeting having listened to what they had to say.
- **Building trust and reducing shame**: *before the meeting* the child/young person is given choices around elements of the meeting, such as where it will be held, who might attend to support them, where everyone should sit; *during the meeting* the child/young person has some control over how they are involved in the meeting, and are able to leave the room as they need to; *after the meeting* the process of having participated and shared in a meeting, and having been responded to in a positive way, can build confidence and encourage the child/young person to actively participate in decisions about their lives.
- **Enabling participation in decision making** *during the meeting* ensuring involvement throughout the meeting, rather than just including children and young people at a point specified for 'the child's voice'; *after the meeting* ensuring that the child/young person understands fully what was discussed, the decisions that were made and the reasons behind them.

Of course, not all children will want to attend meetings. Pölkki et al's (2012) Finnish-based study comprised of semi-structured interviews with eight children aged 7 to 17 in foster care and four interviews with SWs. The researchers reported that children residing in foster care did not always wish to attend meetings; however, they hoped that their SWs would express their views on their behalf. SWs interviewed as part of this study highlighted lack of time as the most significant obstacle to preparatory work with children in care. This research indicates that there are other methods of ensuring children are active participants in their reviews. However, SWs need to be supported practically and emotionally, so they are equipped to gain these views, take them on board and share them at meetings.

It is also important to note that several variables may impact on a child's or young person's ability to meaningfully participate in meeting processes (Thomas, 2015). These may include age, developmental stage, level of ability and previous experiences of participation in meetings. Franklin and Sloper (2009) looked at the participation of disabled children in decisions regarding their care: firstly, by a survey of all social services departments in England to identify the range and nature of disabled children's participation, and secondly, through case studies of six areas to explore the processes and outcomes of participation activity within social care from the points of view of professionals, parents/carers and disabled children. Seventy-six professionals, 24 parents/carers and 21 disabled children aged 5 to 18 were interviewed. The majority of children interviewed had a learning difficulty ranging from mild to severe and six children had a communication impairment. The researchers took different approaches to interviewing, including using photographs, which enabled all participants to be meaningfully included. This study highlighted the need for workers to have a flexible view of what participation is and suggested an individualised approach to participation is required.

Role of professionals

There is very little research that looks at the role of different professionals in helping to ensure that the participation of families and children in social care decision making is meaningful. This is particularly the case for adults.

For children, the importance of a trusting relationship with a dependable professional is key to supporting participation (Schofield and Thoburn, 1996). This is likely also the case for parents. Continuity of relationships is considered vital and it is therefore concerning that frequent changes in SWs are common (Cashmore, 2002). Other professionals are also important to facilitate participation, particularly in meetings. For children, the role of the advocate and that of the IRO are seen as vital to supporting children's right to participation in the context of children's social care meetings.

Advocates

For children, The National Standards for the Provision of Children's Advocacy Services define advocacy as follows:

> Advocacy is about speaking up for children and young people. Advocacy is about empowering children and young people to make sure that their rights are respected and their views and wishes are heard at all times. Advocacy is about representing the views, wishes and needs of children and young people to decision makers, and helping them to navigate the system. (DoH, 1989)

This definition shows why independent advocacy is so important to children's participation. The Adoption and Children Act 2002 (amended Children Act 1989) and The Advocacy Services and Representations Procedure (Children) (Amendment) Regulations 2004 required LAs to make arrangements for advocacy support for children and young people in receipt of social care services who wanted to express their views or make a complaint.

There are a range of advocacy services that operate in the UK for children in care or involved with children's services. For children in care, many statutory services are provided by the voluntary sector and then commissioned by LAs. Advocacy for children can include:

- statutory individual advocacy (provided by charities such as Barnados, NYAS and Coram Voice) or children's rights services delivering individual advocacy services;
- a designated officer for complaints as under section 26A of the Children Act 1989;
- IROs;
- structural advocacy on behalf of children in care by charities such as Become and What Cares? Scotland.

But, while it is widely regarded as important to ensure that children are aware of their right to have an independent advocate, Munro (2001) reported that most children still were not aware of what an advocate was or why they might be important. Even now, there is very little research that looks at how widely advocates are used by children and whether children understand, and value, their role (Stewart and MacIntyre, 2013).

There is clearly a gap in legislation and provision. Sir Martin Narey's fostering stocktake stated that children in foster care should be made aware of their right to advocacy to ensure they become more empowered in the decisions being made about their lives. The report recommended that:

> We therefore believe that it is time to reinforce the statutory guidance 118 that children should know their rights to advocacy and how to access an advocate and urge the DfE to work with the Children's Commissioner and voluntary sector providers of advocacy, including Coram Voice, to ensure this is done. (Narey and Owers, 2018, p 75)

A report by the Office of Children's Commissioner in England (Brady, 2011) found that the introduction of legislation, statutory guidance and policy initiatives has improved children's access to advocacy and that there was greater recognition that children and young people should have the ability to be supported to voice their needs through advocacy. Despite this, research by Ofsted (2010), reported on 1,113 children's knowledge of advocacy, including how to get hold of an advocate, found that 56 per cent said they did know how to contact an advocate and 30 per cent of those interviewed did not know what an advocate was. This does not seem to have improved, with a 2019 Children's Commissioner report finding gaps in organisations about the referral process for advocacy and an under-representation of certain groups in accessing advocacy. Moreover, the report points to pressures on services reducing the availability and quality of the advocacy that is available (Children's Commissioner, 2019).

There are however other reasons that children and young people may not access advocacy. While advocacy may be even more important for children who are not able to communicate themselves, research has found that disabled children and young people are often denied access to advocacy (Oliver et al, 2006). Communication aids can be used to help advocates gain a clear understanding of the child's advocacy needs (Brady, 2011) but the use of these tools is variable (Children's Commissioner, 2019).

Additionally, the role of an advocate can be confusing for a child or young person. While the role of the advocate is to work for children and young people, advocates also have safeguarding duties, which mean they have to break confidentiality if they believe a child is at risk of, or has suffered, significant harm. This could potentially be a barrier to children using or being open with advocates (Lindsey, 1992; Dalrymple, 2004; Pithouse and Crowley, 2007; Boylan and Dalrymple, 2009).

This shows that, while there is a clear argument for advocates to uphold the rights of children and young people through social care decision-making processes and ensure that they have a say, there are many complexities in making this support a reality for all children.

IROs

The child in care review is chaired by an Independent Reviewing Officer. Each of them has a care plan, which must be reviewed on a periodic basis by an independent person, which is an IRO. Their role is to scrutinise the local authority's care plan for the young person and consider the views of the child and other key professionals about the plan. They must challenge the local authority if they believe the plan is not in the best interests of the child.

The views of children and young people regarding their IROs have been gained only recently, possibly in response to recent judgments highlighting ineffective IRO practice through (among other things) failing to gain, understand and take into account the child's views (*R v Rochdale* [2008]; *A and S v Lancs CC* [2012]).

In 2011 a series of national web-based surveys were carried out by the Children's Rights Director (Ofsted, 2011a). The surveys were completed by 50 children between the age of 8 and 17 in 24 different LA areas and they explored children's views of corporate parenting and IROs. This study concluded that young people had little understanding of the role of the IRO, particularly in their responsibility to ensure the child's wishes and feelings are taken into account. Unsurprisingly then, almost 20 per cent of respondents said that no significant decisions were made about their lives in CiC reviews and just 17 per cent felt their IRO listened to them. However, due to the use of quantitative methods, the data collected provide no exploration as to why children and young people held those views.

Similarly, Ofsted (2013) has recently explored the efficacy of the IRO role through reviewing 111 cases in a thematic manner following inspections in ten LAs. Its report draws on evidence from discussions with children in care and with parents, as well as interviews with SMs, a group of IROs, a group of SWs, a group of foster carers and a representative from Children and Family Court Advisory and Support Service (CAFCASS). Findings indicated a general dissatisfaction with reviews among children and the feeling that IROs were not meeting the specifications of their role in terms of participation. The concerns raised in the study are supported in work from Jelicic et al (2014), who conducted a national survey of IROs. Findings suggested that IROs do not feel they have made a contribution to service improvement in terms of ameliorating outcomes for children and young people and that IRO consultation with children was, generally, poor. Jelicic et al (2014) also carried out a study which considered in more depth the IRO role; this was a large study covering four LAs but it did not explicitly consider children's participation in reviews. This study did, however, provide some interesting and insightful data in relation to the importance of reviews being child-centred. It also highlighted children's views of IROs and gave an overview of IRO practice in engaging children. Overall, the study suggested that children's experiences of IROs varied greatly; some had a very positive experience and some a more negative one. The study concluded that the individual IRO was 'fundamental to a child's understanding of their role. If the IROs listened to them without judging, meaningfully involved children in care planning, made sure their voice was heard above all the powerful voices of the professionals, and, above all, made things happen, then children knew IROs were there to make a concrete and positive difference to their lives' (Jelicic et al, 2014, p 39).

The focus upon the efficacy of the IRO role in research indicates a need to establish if SWs' and IROs' views of reviews have changed since the IRO role was introduced in 2002, particularly as conclusions drawn in the studies carried out by Munro (2001), Thomas and O'Kane (1999) and Sinclair (1998) may no longer be relevant. In response, a study undertaken by Pert et al (2014) involved interviewing 25 young people and 17 foster carers to obtain their views of CiC reviews, IROs and participation. However, again, external validity cannot be claimed as the research took place in just one LA. The authors found that few children were offered a genuine opportunity to influence any aspect of their meeting. The reviews were generalised and lacked individuality. Some children did not know who all the attendees were and most reported that they would have preferred fewer people to be present. The authors commented:

> The strength of feeling from the participants in this study confirms that children and young people do not enjoy being part of adult centric decision-making forums. Reviews were enjoyed when they were more child friendly, where they had choice in how they were run and in which they did not feel embarrassed or overwhelmed. (Pert et al, 2014, p 8)

A related action research study carried out by Roesch-Marsh et al (2016) into children's participation and CiC reviews in Scotland surveyed SWs, IROs and young people after 69 review meetings. Follow-up qualitative interviews were then completed with ten young people and a focus group held with the five participating IROs. The study highlighted how young people had mixed feelings about their reviews and the importance of young people being involved and engaged throughout the review process, including preparation for the review, deciding where and when the review was going to take place and who was going to be invited (Roesch-Marsh et al, 2016).

A further study undertaken by Dickens et al (2015) looked at care planning and the role of the IRO in 4 LAs, considering 122 case files of children in care. IROs were given questionnaires as part of the study; these found that 61 per cent cited heavy workloads and time constraints as contributing to them not having the opportunity to visit children to gain their views as much as they would have liked. The case file analysis of the recorded minutes for the most recent review showed that in only 6 per cent of cases IROs had met with the child between reviews. In 42 per cent of cases the IRO had spoken to the child just prior to the review, but given that this was on the same day as the meeting itself, it is questionable how meaningful this would be in terms of participation. It was evident that children had engaged in some form of consultation (for example, through discussions with their SW) in 72 per cent of cases, and overall the views of children were recorded within review minutes in 87 per cent of cases.

This research shows that there are important limitations on the IROs' role and the ability of IROs to carry out their role in a way that enables meaningful participation of children and young people in decision making.

Where next?

Despite progress in children's social care policies, questions remain about the actual implementation of children's and family's rights to participation in decision making, as has been highlighted in the research. This gap between national and international commitment to children's right to participation and the lack of its realisation in practice highlights the challenges faced in balancing participation with non-voluntary intervention. The principle of participation marks and demands a shift to an approach in which children and their families are seen as stakeholders in decisions with a right to some input, rather than a risk factor or in need of protection. The roles of professionals that are in place to support participation are hampered by pressures on LAs and may not provide the support necessary for children and their families. The rest of this book will explore these issues in more depth through a number of research projects that focused on the participation of children and young people in children's social care decision making.

3

How parents and children
view the system

This chapter considers Child Protection Conferences from the perspective of children and parents who have experienced them. National government guidance (*Working Together*, DfE, 2018) states that the overall purpose of a Child Protection Conference is to safeguard children. It aims to ensure children's safety, promote children's health and development and identify when a child is at risk of significant harm. In the United Kingdom, various pieces of legislation, guidance and policies set out the requirements for parents and children to be involved in the process of Child Protection Conferences and for their wishes and feelings to be listened to and considered by professionals. Yet, several research studies show that this is not happening consistently in practice.

In this chapter, I will explore the extent to which children, young people and parents understand the purpose of a Child Protection Conference and whether they feel actively involved in the process. This chapter is based on interviews my colleagues and I carried out across two LAs with 52 parents and 40 children who at the time of the interviews were subject to a Child Protection Plan. The children interviewed were aged between 8 and 18, and all were still living at home with at least one parent.

A Child Protection Conference is a multi-agency forum whereby information relating to the welfare of a child is shared and if the child is deemed to be at risk of significant harm, a Child Protection Plan is implemented or updated. As of March 2018, 53,790 children were subject to Child Protection Plans in England (NSPCC, 2013b). This represents a major increase: a 70 per cent rise in just ten years in the numbers of children subject to a Child Protection Plan in England.

Government guidance (*Working Together*, DfE, 2018) states that professionals should work closely with families to try and increase parents' and children's (in an age-appropriate manner) meaningful participation during the child protection process, encourage joint working and offer support to families. *Working Together to Safeguard Children* (DfE, 2018) states that SWs should ensure children and their parents understand the purpose of the conference, conference reports should be shared with the family well ahead of the meeting and SWs should support the child to attend the Child Protection Conference, or least part of it, if they are mature enough. Previous *Working Together* guidance suggested that most young people who are 12 or over should be invited to conferences, or at least part of them (DfE, 2013b), whereas the current *Working Together* guidance (DfE, 2018) does not stipulate a specific age.

Meaningfully engaging parents in the planning process can be a motivating factor for them and can help them to work in partnership with SWs and other key agencies, which in turn can result in a higher possibility of positive change (Faller, 1981; Wilkins, 2013). Including children in the planning process enables the representation of their perspective of what is taking place:

> Participation by children matters, not only because it is an acknowledgement of their civil rights but because without listening to children and understanding how they experience their world, how can we begin to determine what will ensure their protection and enable them to grow into healthy adults? (Schofield and Thoburn, 1996, p 1)

Organisations are increasingly recognising that, when listened to, children and young people can play a fundamental role in the planning and delivery of services. Government initiatives such as Every Child Matters (2003) and the Children Act 2004 recognise the importance of children's wishes and feelings, married with children's perspectives in planning and intervention (Lancaster, 2010). The Children Act 1989, the Children Act 2004 and the 1990 UNCRC all play significant roles in providing a legal framework for listening to children and parents and recognising the need for the child's voice to be heard in all decision-making processes, including Child Protection Conferences.

Eileen Munro's 2011 report on the child protection system outlined the distinction between 'doing the right thing' for the child (providing children, young people and parents with support to improve their lives) and 'doing things right' (following procedures). The Family Justice Review (2011) was designed to work in tandem with Munro's recommendation for a more child-centred system. The review focused on ensuring that all decisions relating to children and young people should take their wishes and feelings into account, considering their age and level of understanding. It described the need for them to be given age-appropriate explanations relating to the processes affecting them directly. The report highlighted that the child or young person should be supported as early as possible in making their own views known to professionals. However, it is important that children are given a choice about how to communicate their opinions; otherwise, their involvement may be considered tokenistic. For meaningful participation to take place, it is imperative that organisations are committed to genuine, rather than tokenistic, participation, and this applies to Child Protection Conferences. Parents and children need to be given the opportunity to form their own views, as well as a platform to communicate them effectively.

Children's participation

When ascertaining the views and opinions of children and young people, it is paramount that their wishes and feelings can be expressed, listened to by professionals and acted upon wherever possible. Young people should be provided with a safe space and a range of opportunities to participate meaningfully in decision-making forums. This may be verbally by the child or young person or by an advocate, or via drawings, photographs, audio recordings, writing and other visual-based documents (Lancaster, 2007). Creative options such as these promote a necessary forum for the child or young person to express themselves in a manner they feel most comfortable. In addition, a practitioner should promote the formation of a healthy positive relationship with both parents and young people. Research conducted by Milner and Carolin (1999) found children and young people expressed feelings of exclusion regarding their wishes, with SWs failing to listen to them effectively. The importance of a positive and healthy relationship between the SW and child has been highlighted as a significant factor to promote participation; furthermore, children are reliant on their SWs to provide this opportunity for them (Cossar et al, 2011).

Participation can be a protective factor for vulnerable children and young people, leading to increased levels of confidence, self-efficiency and self-worth (Schofield, 2009). However, while the UNCRC (1989) gives children and young people the right to express their views, they are not obligated to participate if they are not willing, and this decision should be respected (Lancaster, 2007). It must be acknowledged that children who have experienced maltreatment may develop feelings of powerlessness (Bell, 2002). In this context, it is all the more important that the child's or young person's feelings and wishes are respected and considered.

The Office of the Children's Commissioner carried out empirical research in 2011, looking into children's and young people's views of the child protection system. Overall, this study found that most children were not clear about the purpose of Child Protection Conferences or the process in general, and they often relied on parents for information about this, rather than professionals with a duty to inform. All the older children interviewed as part of this study had personally attended a conference but, although they had a better understanding of the purpose of the conference than the younger participants, few had seen social work reports or assessments and even fewer had seen their own Child Protection Plans.

Parents

Corby et al (1996) investigated parental participation at Child Protection Conferences. Their findings suggested that parental involvement in the decision-making process was extremely limited and there was a cogent need for this to be expanded. They also agreed the need for changes to be made to the model of Child Protection Conferences to ensure more ethical and effective participation was obtained. Cleaver et al's (2007) studies on children's and parents' experiences of professional intervention likewise highlighted feelings by parents that SWs failed to devote enough time to understanding the families' circumstances, while also failing to listen to their views and opinions. This further reinforces the need for social service professionals to encourage children, young people and parents to express their own individual opinions and views, while assuring them that their wishes will be acted upon wherever possible.

The Child Protection Chair – an independent professional whose responsibility it is to manage the Child Protection Conference – should ensure the meeting is carried out in a way that engages parents and promotes children's and young people's participation (*Working Together*, DfE, 2018). It is good practice for the Chair to meet with the family prior to the conference to establish their understanding of the purpose and the process. The Chair should ensure the child's voice has been considered and that they are given time to express their views and opinions (*Working Together*, DfE, 2018).

Recent research by Featherstone et al (2014) found that, on occasion, childcare SWs adopt an approach they refer to as being 'just there for the child' – focusing on the child, to the exclusion of the wishes and feelings of the child's parents. This approach is not only ethically dubious but also unhelpful in terms of effecting positive change for both children and families more broadly. It can lead to parents feeling blamed and unsupported and it is clearly not in line with the key principles of the Children Act 1989, one of which is working in partnership with parents. The Act also outlines that the needs of children must be the paramount consideration. The combination of these two can ultimately present a challenge for SWs: how should they and other key professionals manage the complex task of working in partnership with parents (who may have abused and neglected their children) while at the same time keeping their ultimate focus on the children? This conundrum represents a key practice issue which many practitioners struggle with.

Understanding and experience of Child Protection Conferences

The research reported here took place in two LAs and involved interviews with 52 parents and 40 children who at the time of interview were subject to a Child Protection Plan. Of the 52 parents, 42 were mothers and 10 were fathers. The 40 children were between the ages of 8 and 17; 22 were girls and 18 were boys. Of the 40 young people interviewed, 12 were between the ages of 8 and 12, and 28 were between 13 and 17 (adolescents). The main questions we aimed to answer were as follows:

- How did young people and parents experience Child Protection Conferences and what were their views of their opportunities to meaningfully participate in these meetings?
- How far did children and parents feel their wishes and feelings were taken into consideration in Child Protection Conferences?
- What were parents' and children's views of SWs and did they feel they made a positive difference to their lives?

Semi-structured interviews were chosen, since they are flexible and allow the interviewer to go in depth on different questions depending on the service users' responses (Thomas, 2003). Furthermore, when working with children and young people, it is important to adopt creative approaches; semi-structured interviews work well with young children because they allow the interviewer to use pictures and tools to help the interviewee to understand the questions being asked and ensure the data being collected are a genuine reflection of their views (Babbie, 2004).

The children and young people who took part in this study were provided with information about the research in an age-appropriate and pictorial format. All the interviews took place within the family home, in familiar surroundings to the participants. The children and young people were offered a choice of methods through which to participate in the interviews. This included the use of pictures to provide a visual representation of a Child Protection Conference, prompting discussion regarding the participant's experiences of these meetings.

During our data analysis the following themes emerged:

- Children's and young people's understanding of Child Protection Conferences was limited.
- The participation of both parents and children in Child Protection Conferences was very limited, indicating that the methods used to engage children and parents in this process were largely ineffective.
- Parents in particular found Child Protection Conferences to be stigmatising and oppressive and they felt powerless before, during and after the meeting.
- Most parents felt unsupported throughout the child protection process, with the majority not feeling positive about their relationships with their SWs.

In combination, these issues have the effect of increasing the likelihood of disengagement from SWs, therefore making it more difficult for families to build positive relationships with SWs and at times with other key agencies. The potential impact on the opportunities for families and professionals to work together to improve the life opportunities for both parents and children is clear.

Views of children and young people on Child Protection Conferences

In both LAs where interviews were conducted for this study, very few children were able to demonstrate a meaningful understanding of a Child Protection Conference or the reason for the meeting taking place. 'Understanding' was rated into two categories: minimal understanding and partial understanding. Ten out of the 40 children interviewed had 'partial understanding'; that is, they had some knowledge of the child protection system but this knowledge was not entirely accurate. These ten were adolescents (ages 13–17), all of whom had personally attended a Child Protection Conference. The other children possessed 'minimal understanding'; that is, they were able to talk about their SWs visiting their home but they did not go to meetings and had no understanding of what took place at any stage.

'They talk about us and how we are doing.' (Female, aged 13)

'They talk about stuff I'm not allowed to hear.' (Female, aged 9)

The majority of children and young people interviewed – 30 of the 40 – did not have a meaningful understanding of the purpose of Child Protection Conferences. None of the children suggested that the purpose of the meetings was to discuss their well-being and safety or make decisions about their life. Children who had personally attended a Child Protection Conference had a better understanding of their function and purpose than those children who had not, but their understanding was still only partial. Of the children who had minimal understanding of the Child Protection Conference, most wanted someone to take the time to explain the purpose of these meetings and crucially the outcome of the meeting. When we asked the children whom they would like to explain the process and outcome, most stated their parents, though two said they would like their SW to do this.

Out of the 40 young people interviewed, only 13 had personally attended a Child Protection Conference. Eight of the young people had an advocate to support them through the process, but most of the participants did not feel prepared or supported. Some reported a negative experience of attending a conference:

'I felt prepared, but it was not a good experience. I prepared myself and thought I would have a say. Afterwards I stormed out crying and never went back. The Chair asked me a question then shut me off. I felt the professionals were there for my mum … not to support us.' (Female, aged 16)

'I was told to "shut up" in a conference once by my social worker. I feel I get an input but feel like I'm the mediator between my social worker and my parents.' (Female, aged 17)

'I was worried about coming off the "at risk" register. I was assured there would be support, but there wasn't. I phoned the social worker, no answer. I felt my opinion did not matter. I couldn't speak at the conference.' (Female, aged 15)

All the young people who attended the conference reported that they had only been allowed to attend one part of the meeting, generally the start, and none had been informed of the agreed action plan arising out of the meeting. None were able to identify any of the meeting's actions or goals. The children described feeling disappointed by the lack of communication demonstrated by professionals and deemed the meeting to be 'a waste of time', as they were not informed of the ways in which their situation would change. Thirty-eight of the young people had not seen a report related to the meeting. For those who had seen a report or assessment, this was linked to their attendance of a Child Protection Conference. Only two adolescents had seen all or part of a social work report or assessment. Neither report had been shared by a SW: one was shared with the child by a teacher at their school and the other report was read through by a young person following the meeting:

> 'I read through the report myself, the social worker didn't go through it with me and I found it very confusing. I only read one though as my mum said I shouldn't because it will upset me.' (Female, aged 13)

One point of interest which arose from this study, and one which is a new finding that has not been raised in previous research, was that 30 of the 40 young people interviewed stated that things had been difficult at home straight after the conference. When discussing what had happened after the meeting, the young people made the following comments:

> '… mum was upset after the meeting and it made me feel bad to see her so upset.' (Female, aged 12)

> '… there was a poor feeling in the house after the meeting.' (Male, aged 9).

> 'After the conference we were all over the place, mum was stressed and we all got upset.' (Female, aged 14)

This raises issues about the way in which SWs and other professionals support families in the period following conferences. It is particularly pertinent when considering the aftermath of conferences taking place on a Friday afternoon, a practice which occurred regularly in both of these LAs.

Parents' views of Child Protection Conferences

We asked parents about their understanding of a Child Protection Plan, core group meeting, Child Protection Conference and social work report. Most parents had heard of each meeting or assessment and understood their purpose, though one parent had not heard of a social work report. All the parents interviewed had attended a Child Protection Conference, but the majority did not feel prepared for it, especially the initial conference.

> 'The first conference was terrifying; I didn't know what was happening.' (Female, aged 42)

> 'I wanted more support for the initial conference; I felt blindfolded … like a lamb being led to slaughter.' (Female, aged 41)

> 'I was told of an allegation one day before the conference and I had no time to get a solicitor.' (Female, 27)

Parents were asked if the discussions during the conference were easy to understand and follow. The majority said that they were, but five parents felt that the language and terminology used by the professionals made things unclear. We asked the parents if they were able to express their views and say everything that was important to them during the conference. Again, the majority of parents said that they were able to do this. However, this mainly occurred when they were asked a direct question by the Chair; parents suggested that they rarely initiated a discussion. Some parents said that they had to fight to be heard and felt that their words were misconstrued:

> 'I had to scream and shout, I raised my voice but it's just natural to have to do that during a conference.' (Female, aged 29)

> 'There were so many people there (in the conference) that I felt intimidated. People talked over me or twisted what I said.' (Female, aged 43)

> 'There is too much authority in one room on one person. It's intimidating, no-one is the perfect parent. I felt like a rabbit in the headlights. They didn't understand my point

of view and didn't listen. I gave up in the end.' (Female, aged 41)

Parents were asked how they felt at the end of a conference. Forty-eight of the 52 parents described the experience in a negative way, using words and statements such as 'emotional', 'tearful', 'upset', 'frustrated', 'not listened to', 'relieved it was over', 'intimidated', 'stressed', 'waste of time', 'angry' and 'confused':

'It makes you feel like a school kid and inferior.' (Female, aged 44)

'I felt like I was being put into a corner.' (Female, aged 41)

'I was worn out. It is traumatic.' (Female, aged 43)

'I feel like whatever I say in a meeting is disregarded.' (Female, aged 32)

Most parents did not like the degree of personal information about them being shared in front of so many people, many of whom they did not know. Parents found it very difficult that such personal information – much of which they said was inaccurate or very out of date – was disseminated through the social work reports. They stated that a combination of the oppressive reports and the meetings themselves made them feel embarrassed and that they were being shamed about their situation. Most parents reported feelings of powerlessness and stated that they found conferences to be a very intimidating experience. A majority of the parents stated they had found out too late that they could bring someone to support them at the initial Child Protection Conference. Most parents stated that the third or fourth conference was less intimidating in part as they knew they were allowed to bring someone and in part as they knew the process and format better by then.

Different reports and assessments were shared with parents throughout the child protection process, but how these were shared varied hugely depending on their individual SW. The majority of the parents reported that they only saw the social work report for the Child Protection Conference either the day before the meeting or on the day of the meeting itself. Those who saw it the day before the meeting tended to receive it through the post (rather than in person from the SW), and this added to their anxiety as they did not have a chance to discuss it prior to the meeting with the SW. Some described that the SW met with them briefly before the conference, rushing through explanations of the process or report:

> 'Sometimes they were sent out in the post late. One social worker went through it with me on the day of the conference.' (Female, aged 29)

Nearly all the parents wanted the SW to share reports and assessments well in advance of the conference and to take time in discussing the report and the process with them. One parent did express a wish to have the assessment sent to them via post, though it transpired this was due to the negative relationship they had with their SW.

> 'I want a face-to-face discussion and a copy of the report, but there is pressure to make a comment straight away and I need time to digest it so I can make an informed decision.' (Female, aged 31)

> 'Someone should come out and sit with you to go through it, it is an awful lot to take in.' (Female, aged 43)

> 'I want someone to come and share it with me face-to-face and explain it to me properly, so it doesn't feel so rushed. Sometimes the social worker comes just to get me to sign it and is gone again within 10 minutes.' (Female, aged 44)

Complaint procedures

The complaints system plays an integral role in social work practice, ensuring as it does that procedures are updated, assessed accordingly, and the wishes of children and parents are considered and brought forward. This subject will be covered in depth in Chapter 7.

Out of the 40 children interviewed, only 5 said they had been told about the complaint process. Of these 5, 2 of the older children had made a complaint and had experienced a positive change as a result: one adolescent was allocated a different SW, while the other found a change in the way their SW interacted with them:

> 'My social worker used to be really horrible to me but after the complaint she started being nicer.' (Male, aged 12)

The remaining 35 children said that they had never been given the opportunity to make a complaint, and even if they had wished to do so, they did not know who to complain to. Some children reported feeling scared, as they were uncertain of the implications to themselves and their family if they were to complain. This point is considered further in Chapter 7.

Parents had a similar response; many described the consequences of making a complaint. They felt that it would not make a difference to their situation and could potentially even make things worse. Eleven out of 40 parents had been told how to make a complaint, of whom 3 had made a complaint to children's services about their SW. Two of these parents reported being happy with the outcome.

Relationships with SWs

Views of children and young people

The 40 children and young people interviewed as part of this study had very mixed views of SWs. The split between broadly positive and broadly negative views was 50:50. It was clear that the children were considerably more positive about their SWs than their parents were. The following are some of the positive accolades which were used to describe SWs: 'helpful', 'they listen', 'understanding', 'trusting', 'makes things better', 'reliable' and 'approachable'.

The children who had formulated a strong relationship with their SW felt positive about their experience:

'I feel I have someone to talk to, I can call them if I'm upset or worried about anything.' (Female, aged 14)

'I felt like I had someone to speak to and could let my worries out. They are there when you need them.' (Female, aged 13)

'She has helped my mum with her drinking, she has made the environment safer for me and my brother. I feel safer now.' (Female, aged 12)

'The social worker was kind and friendly and was always on time and she was a good listener. I wish my social worker had more time to spend with me, getting to know me and what I like and don't like.' (Female, aged 10)

Children who had not built a positive relationship with their SW were a lot more negative in their description, using words such as 'bossy', 'doesn't listen', 'nosey', 'annoying', 'doesn't tell me what's happening', 'they cancel' and 'is always late':

> 'They made me feel depressed, I won't speak to them. They haven't helped, they just make things worse. You say something to them, and they make it out to be ten times worse than it is.' (Female, aged 17)

> 'I don't like talking to her, she talks too much and for too long.' (Male, aged 11)

> 'The social worker comes with their own agenda, she is always looking for things to back up her view, it feels like the social worker is writing her own movie about our lives. We [the interviewee and her siblings] always asked if we could attend core groups and conferences, but we were always told by the social worker that this was inappropriate. The social worker used her power to put us onto a Child Protection Plan but we were not listened to and things were completely out of control. The social worker is rude and says inappropriate things like "I can make this as easy or as difficult as I want".' (17-year-old female with 12- and 14-year-old siblings)

Those children who described their SW in positive terms reported having a better relationship with them. Overall, they felt their SWs had assisted in promoting a change to their family life: their home lives had improved, and things were generally better since SWs had become involved with their families.

The children and young people who described their SWs in negative terms felt as though their involvement was a waste of time and that nothing had changed since the SW's work had commenced. A small number said that SWs had made things more difficult for them and their families. Interestingly, the parents of the children who described having a negative relationship with their SW tended to share their child's views. This seems to indicate that a child's perception of their SW often depends on their parents' perception and, accordingly, the relationship the SW has with their parents; if the SW treated their parents in an honest and respectful manner, children were more likely to be positive about them.

Parents' views

A majority of the parents (43 of the 52 interviewed) described having a poor relationship with their child's SW and used negative words and statements to describe them: *'undermining'*, *'dishonest'*, *'contradicting'*, *'twists what I say'*, *'misunderstood my problems'*, *'doesn't explain what is happening'*, *'nosey'*, *'cancels'* and *'always late'*. The nine remaining parents were positive about social work involvement and found SWs to be *'approachable'* and *'trustworthy'*.

> 'The social worker always keeps me updated in everything and I feel really included.' (Female, aged 28)

> 'The social worker pulls everyone together and does the best for the children. It is the hardest job in the world.' (Male, aged 50)

During the interview process, many children and parents reported a regular change of SW and varying degrees of professional input and involvement. This was clearly a significant issue for them, creating a barrier in the formation of a positive relationship between the family and the SW. It seemed that in both LAs there was a very high turnover of SWs, and even when the SW did not change due to staff retention issues they would sometimes do so as a result of LA structures. For example, for the first few months families in both LAs would work with a SW from the Duty and Assessment Team, then they would move on to a SW from the Child Protection Community Team. A number of parents and children stated that the rapid rotation of SWs made it very difficult for them to build up a positive working relationship with their SW, and this impacted on their ability to trust the SW and also led them to feel hopeless, demotivated and angry. Some parents even stated that this led to them not allowing SWs into their homes. Both parents and young people related that SWs would often leave without saying goodbye and they would never see them again – they would just be allocated a new SW who would visit a few weeks later and they would have to start the process again. Many of the parents and young people expressed feeling very upset about having to discuss their personal business with so many different people and also about there not being a proper handover from one SW to another. Some parents and young people reported having up to eight or nine SWs in a year.

'I have had so many social workers. I have had about 8 in the last 14 months.' (Female, aged 35)

Many of the parents stated that, overall, communication with the SWs had been very poor and that they had found them hard to reach. There is an irony here; SWs talk about 'hard to reach' or 'hard to engage parents' but perhaps there is also an issue with hard to reach SWs.

Parents reported that they would often be 'told off' or spoken to in a patronising way by SWs; for example, quite a few of the parents stated that they had attended the conference with their younger children as they did not have anyone to look after them but had then been told that it was not acceptable to bring their children. This made parents feel very frustrated: they had already told the SWs that they did not have anyone to look after their children, but the SWs seemed to struggle to understand or empathise with their predicament.

Many of the parents interviewed were extremely negative in their views towards SWs, although separately they demonstrated an awareness that SWs are very busy.

'The social worker was quite stretched, she didn't really have time to spend with the children. My children also say [the social worker] has not spent any time getting to know the family, however they do not blame her for this, they know she is really busy.' (Female, aged 37)

Some of the language used by parents when speaking about SWs was very forthright:

'… the previous social worker would downplay and dismiss my anxieties about the child protection process – she often did not pick up the phone when I called and she did not call back and she would just tell me not to worry and it made me feel as if I was making a fuss.' (Female, aged 32)

'The social worker is very condescending and talks to me like I am two. She second-guesses everything and treats me like I am five. Having a social worker is very negative, they give me deadlines and when I do them, they give me new deadlines. I know it sounds harsh but my current social worker is atrocious.' (Male, aged 35)

'I have never been listened to by social workers. ... They should provide reassurance and spend time to build up trust necessary for good relationships rather than being unreliable, rude and oppressive.' (Female, aged 37)

'I have been calling for weeks because my daughter needs help then I get messages to cancel so many times, she keeps putting me off. They come up with a plan but none of what they [social workers] say they are going to do happens. Social services were supposed to help me get everything up together but nothing happened.' (Female, aged 42)

'The social worker needs better people skills; the kids don't find her friendly and she is not approachable. Not so warm with the kids. That affects how they are around her. She makes us all feel like we are the naughty school children.' (Male, aged 34)

Children's and parent's participation in Child Protection Conferences

The extent of understanding children displayed of child protection processes was largely age-related. *Working Together to Safeguard Children* (DfE, 2018) states that children of sufficient age, depending on their development, should be invited to conferences. However, within the confines of our research, very few children had attended a conference, which suggests that even older children who should have been given this opportunity are not actively involved in the process or even encouraged to take part. Although children who are mature enough should be given the opportunity to be involved, it should not be assumed that all children will want to participate in this process, and indeed within our research, seven children indicated that they did not wish to take part.

The lack of knowledge of the child protection process demonstrated by children and young people in this study supports earlier findings on this topic, such as those highlighted by Cossar et al (2011). The majority of children interviewed were not clear about the purpose of a Child Protection Conference; few children had attended a conference and even fewer had seen a social work assessment or report. Older children had a better understanding of the child protection process, as did those children who had personally experienced a conference. Cossar et al (2011) found that children who attended a Child

Protection Conference described them as 'difficult'; they felt that they were not listened to by professionals and were under-prepared. This was also confirmed by our study. Only 6 out of 26 children in the study by Cossar et al (2011) had seen all or part of their assessment or report, compared to 2 children from our study, both of whom were older children. Cossar et al (2011) found that younger children were able to identify aspects of the child protection process but struggled to understand the reason for social work involvement due to limited information being provided to them. Again, this accorded with the findings in our study, which found that younger children in particular had minimal understanding of the reasons for social work involvement. In both this study and that of Cossar et al (2011), children expressed not feeling listened to during conferences or described negative experiences throughout the entire process. The need for children to be effectively supported and prepared for this highly stressful and emotional process should therefore be clear; currently, it is an oppressive experience for children and young people.

SWs should share information with children and young people, while providing support for them to understand assessments and reports (Bell, 2002; Cleaver et al, 2004). This should be done in an accessible manner, promoting the enablement of children in understanding what is taking place in their lives. Yet it was discovered in our research that only two reports had been shared, by a teacher and a parent. A large number of parents complained that the SW had hurriedly shared the report with them on the day of the conference, thus failing to allow sufficient time for the parent(s) to fully understand the information, challenge any inaccuracies and analyse the contents sufficiently.

All the parents within our research wanted the SW to share the report with them prior to the conference, and at least three days in advance, as local guidance suggests. Four parents wanted to read through the report themselves; this highlights the importance of recognising and respecting individual differences (BASW, 2012). LAs should also ensure that reports for Child Protection Conferences are shared with children and young people in advance of the meeting, in an age-appropriate manner. Consideration should be given to how such reports are communicated. Furthermore, the Child Protection Chair should dedicate time to meeting with the child or young person prior to the meeting to discuss the process and listen to their wishes and feelings.

The outcome of these meetings needs to be shared with the children, young people and parents. From our research, it became evident that this was not taking place; using Hart's 'ladder' of participation (1992), this would be viewed as 'manipulation'. Lancaster (2007) discussed the importance of including children from the very beginning of social work involvement – from planning to evaluation – so as to encourage feelings of inclusion and provide children with the ability to genuinely participate. However, many children within this research study had minimal understanding of the child protection process. Thus, for them to contribute to a plan that they do not understand might prove difficult or indeed impossible. Furthermore, this study found that children are not included in the evaluation process; none of the children interviewed knew the outcome of their Child Protection Conference or were able to identify any of the objectives of their Child Protection Plan.

It is imperative that SWs and Child Protection Chairs work together to promote participation within the conference for all the attendees. However, the parents interviewed as part of this study described feelings of intimidation in the conference, and 42 of the parents had experienced negative feelings during and straight after the conference. This clearly indicates that there is a need for support for parents in the period immediately following a Child Protection Conference. This will ensure that parents have understood the discussion and the outcome and that they are provided with a space to discuss any further worries or concerns. Parents leaving a Child Protection Conference with high levels of agitation or frustration potentially places vulnerable children at further risk of harm, due to a likelihood of emotional over-reaction to what has taken place (Muench et al 2017).

A further issue raised by several parents related to the number of people who were invited to the conference; often they did not know who they were or why they were there. Some parents stated that at the initial conference the local children's centre manager had attended but they had never worked with them before or had no contact with them after the meeting, so they did not understand why they were there. Many parents also said that they did not understand why the police were there; this was never explained to them and in turn made them feel more uncomfortable.

Children and parents: their wishes and views

Munro (2011) highlights the importance of carrying out direct work with children so as to gain an understanding of children's wishes and feelings and to create a 'child-centred' system. However, this can be difficult when children are reluctant to discuss their feelings due to a fear of an escalation in problems or that sharing their feelings will result in negative reactions by their parents after the SW is no longer there (O'Quigley, 2000). SWs aim to see children alone to avoid this issue and to build a positive rapport, encouraging an open and honest discussion related to their wishes and feelings.

Findings from our research indicated that very few children had attended a Child Protection Conference. Most felt they were not listened to and their wishes and feelings were not considered during the meeting or process. Some of the children had limited understanding of a Child Protection Conference, thus making it difficult to measure whether their wishes and feelings had been ascertained by the SW prior to the conference. Children require the opportunity to be prepared prior to the conference and given realistic expectations of what the experience will entail; more emphasis should be placed on SWs and Child Protection Chairs to ensure this happens.

The use of advocates has been shown to be effective for children and young people during the Child Protection Conference (Barnes, 2012). In our research, nearly a third of the children interviewed who had attended a Child Protection Conference were supported by an advocate, and these children were more positive about their experiences of the conference. This highlights the importance of representation for children in some capacity, to ensure their wishes and feelings are heard.

Parents who had a positive relationship with their SW felt their wishes and feelings were considered during the conference. However, unfortunately, most parents felt that although they were able to express their opinions and say everything that was important to them, this did not necessarily indicate that they felt that their wishes and feelings were considered. Parents had little choice about who attended the conference and where it was held, although some did report being able to express a preference about the time the conference took place, with reports of the meeting being rearranged if they were unable to attend. All the parents interviewed wished for fewer professionals to attend the conference, especially from schools – but most understood the reason for their attendance and the importance of this requirement.

Those children who described attaining a positive relationship with their SW also reported fewer negative feelings about the child protection process. Cossar et al (2011) describe how integral it is for a child to have a positive relationship with their SW. This was also identified as a corresponding theme throughout our research. A trusting and positive relationship with a SW can assist in developing in the child feelings of inclusion and participation. Children demonstrated awareness of how professionals viewed their parents, and, in turn, how their parents viewed the professionals. If the relationship between a SW and a parent is strained, it is likely the child will have a view similar to that of their parent; this makes it considerably more difficult for the SW to build a trusting relationship with the child and in turn leads to reduced participation by the child.

Children and young people must be involved in the child protection process and should feel able to make informed choices and decisions about their life, with the support from their SW. Butler-Sloss (1988) suggests that children engage better with SWs who dedicate time to building a rapport with the child, by listening to them rather than bombarding them with questions.

Both children and parents within our study identified the high numbers of SWs that had been involved in their life and expressed their desire for this to be reduced. It was felt this regular change made it difficult for parents and children to build up a positive relationship with their SW. Staff retention in the social work profession has been widely reported as a significant difficulty. Recruitment and retention of experienced SWs has been reported to be a challenge faced by LAs across the country (Baginsky, 2013), and experiencing a change in SW is a reality faced by many families who use services.

Summary

The primary aim of this chapter was to outline parents' and children's experiences of Child Protection Conferences and SWs. Many of the children interviewed as part of this study were not clear about the purpose of a Child Protection Conference and had minimal participation in the process. It is of interest that little has changed regarding children's and young people's views and experiences of the child protection process since the findings reported by the Office of the Children's Commissioner (Cossar et al, 2011). This is despite the recent changes to policy and guidance, which have reiterated the importance of the 'voice of the child'. Both children and parents from our study described Child Protection Conferences as a negative experience, with most parents describing the process as stigmatising and part of a 'blame game'.

Half of the children interviewed in this study viewed social work involvement in a positive light and felt their SW had made a positive difference to their family life. Although most parents did not take the same view as their children, some parents were appreciative of the help they had received from children's services. However, the majority of the parents interviewed were very negative about their experiences of both SWs and Child Protection Conferences.

Many of the children and parents within our study were not informed on the process of making a complaint, if they wished to do so. Boylan and Dalrymple (2011) stress the importance of children being able to access complaint procedures to strengthen their position. The complaint process can also encourage the restructuring of certain procedures, resulting in better methods of practice being implemented. Service users need to feel empowered and have control over their lives; knowing that they can make a complaint provides an important sense of control.

The Children Act 1989 and Munro's report (2011) highlight the importance of engaging children and young people in the child protection system to ensure their voices are heard, yet in practice this does not seem to be happening. The children and young people in this study had rarely attended conferences, and when they did, they did not feel listened to or supported and demonstrated minimal or partial understanding of the process.

Children and parents need to be better informed regarding the process of a Child Protection Conference, and such information needs to be provided in an accessible format. The process should be explained in a clear way, with reports and assessments tailored to each individual and shared in advance of the conference. Child Protection Chairs need to meet with parents and young people prior to the conference to ensure they understand the purpose of such meetings and to allow their views to be shared. SWs need to be supportive throughout the process and explain the purpose of meetings and reports and also how they think this process will help improve things for both children and parents.

4

Young people's perspectives

Introduction

The importance of enabling vulnerable children and young people to participate in decisions which affect them cannot be underestimated. Research has shown that participation acts as a protective factor for this group and increases feelings of confidence, self-efficiency and self-worth (Dickens et al, 2015). It is hard to disagree with the view expressed by Schofield and Thoburn (1996) on this subject:

> Participation by children matters, not only because it an acknowledgment of their civil rights but because without listening to children and understanding how they experience their world, how can we begin to determine what will ensure their protection and enable them to grow into healthy adults? (Schofield and Thoburn, 1996, p 1)

Promoting effective and meaningful participation for young people and parents should be at the core of social work practice; much turns on the quality of the relationship between the SW and the child, especially since the child is wholly reliant on professionals to provide the opportunity for participation (Cossar et al, 2011). Previous research into young people's views of IROs and reviews (for example, Jelicic et al, 2014; Roesch-Marsh et al, 2016) adds weight to this argument.

This chapter focuses on what children and young people in care have identified as being important to them in terms of their participation in the CiC review process, what the potential barriers might be and where we might go next to improve the opportunities of children and young people to participate in decisions made about their own lives. Consideration will be given to a range of research relating to this crucial issue while focusing on two studies I was directly involved with and which specifically asked these questions. These studies gathered the views of a total of 35 children and young people aged 8–17 years, all of whom were 'in care' of two LAs in the years 2014 and 2018. Pseudonyms have been used for the young participants throughout.

Our initial exploration of these issues involved research interviews with 25 young people between the ages of 8 and 17 in Local Authority One and it highlighted a number of key issues. It was evident that the young participants lacked a basic understanding about the purpose of review meetings. They reported low levels of involvement in meetings logistics, for example, location of meeting, who was invited to the meeting and what as on the agenda. Although almost all children (23) knew they had regular review meetings, their understanding of the purpose of reviews varied a great deal:

> 'They are there to check up on me.' (Young woman, aged 14)

> 'I think it's to do with school.' (Boy, aged 8)

> 'They are to see how things are going.' (Boy, aged 10)

None of the young people interviewed stated that the meetings were to review the care plan or make decisions about their lives, although one child did suggest that review meetings were to look forward to the next six months. Participants had mixed views of the review meetings: eight said they were 'OK' about their meetings, nine found them too long and dull. Just two felt that meetings were positive:

> 'I like the meetings, I like to have a chat and it's nice to talk about me.' (Boy, aged 10)

Some young people reported stronger and more negative feelings:

> 'The meetings themselves are a bit scary, they are a bit daunting really, so when I am not in the right frame of mind to talk about anything it's just … embarrassing.' (Young man, aged 15)

For the majority of the young people the content of the meetings was repetitive, boring and lacked any individuality or creativity:

> 'It just tell us about school, how's school? Tell me about your health, are you happy? Tell me about school.' (Young woman, aged 13)

Relationships were felt to be key and many of the young people were very positive about their IROs, although there was often a lack of clarity over what the role should and did entail. Therefore, while it was clearly positive that young people felt they were able to trust their IROs, their positive viewpoints may have been influenced by a lack of clarity over what they should have expected from their IROs in terms of how often they visited and the holistic element to their role which involves more than just chairing their meetings on a six-monthly basis. Relationships with SWs were often more challenging for young people and the quality of relationships had significant impact on children and young people's sense of control and satisfaction with services generally as well as with reviews and the decisions taken by children's services. Many of the young people interviewed experienced fairly regular changes of SWs and this impacted on their ability to build up a relationship and trust their SWs.

In terms of the long-term benefits of children in care reviews, young people felt largely detached from any tangible positive or negative effect upon their lives. Only two participants could remember any action points or goals agreed at reviews. Adolescents felt particularly dissociated from the outcomes of their reviews, with many having high levels of dissatisfaction or apathy:

> 'What's the point, nothing ever changes so there is no point.'
> (Young woman, aged 16)

Lack of choice and control in who attended reviews was one of the most emotive topics for children and young people. One child counted nine adults at her last review, and when asked whom she would like to attend her next review she removed five of them. This was not unusual; only a small number of young people were comfortable with the amount of professionals who attended their reviews:

> 'At my last review random people started turning up and
> I was like who are you? I didn't know who they were, it
> was crap.' (Young man, aged 16)

Young people felt confused about some of the people who attended reviews; one group of three siblings thought their foster carers' SW was their SW's friend.

The research in Local Authority One reached the conclusion that, to a great extent, review meetings tended to meet the needs of the professionals involved more than the children and young people. We concluded that to enable young people to be more involved in their reviews and make the meetings meaningful for the people at the heart of this process, SWs and IROs need to prioritise preparation time with the young people who they were working with. Young people needed to be much more actively involved in deciding who attended the review, where it took place, what was discussed at the review (the agenda) and when the review took place.

So was the situation any different in Local Authority Two? In this LA we interviewed ten more young people aged 8–17 to revisit these issues and gather their views on the extent to which they felt involved in decision making and the review process. Pseudonyms are used throughout. One of the major issues with all the ten young people interviewed as part of this study was that they had all experienced a very high turnover of SWs, with some young people having had over seven SWs in a year.

One of the major barriers to fostering positive working relationships between young people and SWs is the high turnover of SWs in many LAs' children's services departments, an issue which was identified by the Munro Review (2012) and more recently by Research in Practice. The average childcare SW leaves frontline practice after only two to three years in practice (Bowyer and Roe, 2015). When compared to the average period that individuals stay in social work more generally – eight years – this statistic gives some indication as to the challenging nature of this area of work. To put this in context, the average period of practice for teachers is 15 years, nurses 16 years, and doctors 25 years (Bowyer and Roe, 2015). It was striking to discover that in a recent Ofsted inspection of the LA where I conducted my fieldwork, nearly half of the SWs in the frontline teams were found to have less than two years post-qualifying experience (Ofsted, 2017 – details anonymised to protect confidentiality of fieldwork site).

The picture looks even bleaker when we consider research by the Association of Directors of Children's Services (ADCS, 2016), which has shown that the turnover of SWs in children's services has increased significantly in recent years. As a result, young people, particularly those in 'care' who experience social work services over a number of years, often have a high number of case workers during their period of engagement with social services. It may seem that as soon as they get to know their SW and feel comfortable engaging with them, the SW is replaced with someone new and they have to begin the process again. The implications for participation and engagement in this context are clear.

The final compounding factor relating to this issue is the organisational structures within LAs themselves. Children moving through the care system are dealt with by different teams during particular phases of their period in care – for example, child protection and court teams, looked after children teams, and leaving care teams – which mean that continuity of professional input cannot be guaranteed.

When conducting interviews as part of this study, we first set about establishing the number of SWs each of the participants of the study had had, before going on to explore how this may have impacted on their relationship with their current SW and, more broadly, their feelings of engagement with the review process. It is important to note at this juncture that in contrast to SWs, the turnover rate for IROs is low. The continuity this affords potentially means that IROs are able to offer greater stability to the children and young people they support (Dickens et al, 2015). I was particularly interested to discover whether this was the case in practice for the participants in this study.

The accounts of the children and young people were reviewed and their content organised by the following themes:

1. the number of SWs/IROs each young person had;
2. the young people's views of IROs;
3. the young people's views of SWs;
4. the young people's perceptions of the review meetings (including who decided the agenda, who was invited and when and where the review took place).

The following sections take each of these themes in turn to frame the discussion around children's and young people's views of reviews.

What is the relationship between a high number of SWs/IROs and a young person's level of engagement?

Changes to their designated SW – both prior to and during their time in care – was an experience that all of the participants in this study shared. It was clear that having so many different SWs had impacted on their trust in the profession and reduced opportunities for them to form meaningful relationships with their SWs. For example, Charmaine said that she had had one IRO during the last two years and three SWs during her time in care, but 'probably about 20' SWs in her whole life.

Some of the participants, such as Josh, couldn't remember how many SWs they had had – there had been so many. This is a concerning finding and one which was also present in previous studies in this area (Muench et al, 2017).

On average, the participants said they had three or four SWs per year – many more than the number of IROs. Apart from one young person who had two IROs, all of the other participants had only one IRO the whole time they were in care. Eight of the participants expressed that the consistency this relationship provided was important to them. This accords with recent research (Dickens et al, 2015). Katy reflected on her experience thus:

> 'One thing I will say is an IRO is the one person who was consistently there from day one. I had her from day one of coming into care on my very first review, all the way through.'

A key part of the SW's role is to prepare young people for their reviews; this responsibility is outlined in the *IRO Handbook* (DfES, 2010). If a young person experiences regular changes in SW, this will likely impinge upon the ability of the SW whose ultimate responsibility it is to prepare them for their review, because the SW is less likely to have had a long-term relationship with the young person. It was troubling to learn that some of the young people in this study had only met with their SW once prior to the review meeting. The impact of this is felt by SWs too; those interviewed for this study also lamented that on occasion they had hardly met with the young person prior to the review. For those young people who enjoyed a positive relationship with their IRO or/and SW (although it was more common that they had positive relationships with their IROs), it was clear that they were more engaged in the review process and found them to be more meaningful. This echoes the findings of previous studies by Pert et al (2014), Jelicic et al (2014) and Roesch-Marsh et al (2016).

Another theme which came through in the interviews was that the consistency provided by IROs was very different to that provided by SWs. For example, Katy had five different SWs between the ages of 12 and 17, but retained the same IRO throughout this time. Tyrone spoke highly of the positive relationship he had formed with his IRO, in sharp contrast to his experience with a rapid succession of different SWs:

> 'I didn't have a good relationship with any of my SWs up to that point. The SWs always kept changing so I never really got to know them. So, the only person I could really

speak to at that point was my IRO or my foster carer. So whenever we saw the IRO we would put everything on her to sort out.'

Here, Tyrone is clearly voicing his faith in the IRO's ability to resolve his issues, in contrast with that of his SWs who he 'never really got to know'. Many of the other young people in this study positioned the IRO as a consistent 'voice of reason' in their lives. Chloe described hers as a 'saviour', and she, Mason and Katy all reported that their IRO had helped to change things for them in a positive way. When probed, examples given of this 'change' were seemingly small things like ensuring appointments with the doctor or dentist took place. Chloe, Mason and Katy all said that when it came to the more significant things – for example, resolving complex issues such as family contact – their IRO seemed ineffective. This will be discussed further later in this chapter.

One of the young people interviewed in this study, Kiera, reported that she had such a poor relationship with one of her SWs that she would refuse to meet with her and would choose to either leave the house or stay in her room when this particular individual visited. When the responsibility for preparing a young person for their review lies with the SW, the quality of relationship between SW and child has a direct impact on how the young person engages in the review meeting. Despite the difficulties caused by numerous changes of SWs, it was heartening to hear examples of the young people who had formed a bond with one SW in particular over the period of their time in care. This was an experience which had clearly stayed with that young person. In these examples, the young people described how this experience allowed them to place their trust in the SW in question:

> 'There was one social worker from before when I was young when my dad said he wanted to punch her so for ages I got confused and thought social workers were for punching and bad but I don't think that now. I like my social worker now – she talks to me normally; she comes in her car which is a treat. She is friendly, she creates a good atmosphere, she is always cheerful and happy.' (Jordan)

Katy also described forming a bond with one particular SW:

Clive: Have you had any good social workers?
Katy: Um, one.

Clive:	Okay.
Katy:	At the time I think I said I hated her … but now that I'm older I realise that I didn't actually. She kind of got me on a boundary level.

So although the number of SWs young people have during their engagement with children's services is clearly important, it seems that the personal attributes of the individual SW are key to whether they feel able to trust them. What came across in this interview, as with many of the others, was that regardless of how many SWs a young person has over a period of time, they are able to build up a positive working relationship if the SW is friendly, listens to them and treats them with respect – ultimately, if they are 'human'. Many of us would consider these qualities to be the bare minimum we would expect from a SW, so it is worrying to hear that at times the young people did not feel they had been treated in this manner. We will explore further the relationship between the young people and their IROs and their SWs in the following two sections.

Young people's views of IROs

Eight of the participants in this study said that they had a good working relationship with their IRO. For example, Emma described building up a positive rapport with her IRO:

Clive:	Do you feel like you built up a bit of a relationship with the IRO or not really?
Emma:	A little bit. There was a time when like after the review – because my foster carers were telling her how I do drama and stuff like that, and there was another thing that she told her – and she was like 'Oh can I come to your room and have a look?' So we did and we just sat there and chatted for a bit and it was nice but like informal and stuff like that. Yeah, so I'd say a little bit, a little bit of a relationship, yeah, 'cos she was bonkers and I liked that!

Emma's response highlights the importance of adaptability in IROs and SWs towards young people and their individual circumstances, a skill which enables them to relate to children and young people on a human level rather than within the confines of a formal professional-client relationship.

One of the barriers to building up a relationship between a young person and their IRO is the lack of regularity in contact; all the young participants said that they only saw their IRO at the review meeting or for a brief catch-up beforehand. In practice, this meant that unless the young person moved placement and required an extra review, they would only see their IRO twice a year. This reality seems at odds with the guidance set out in the *IRO Handbook*, which states that there are now two clear and separate aspects to the function of the IRO:

i. chairing the child's review; and
ii. monitoring the child's case on an ongoing basis. (DfES, 2010, p 11)

We have to ask how effective or even feasible the monitoring of a child's case on an ongoing basis can be without the IRO seeing that child between reviews. Under Regulation 36 the IRO is required to speak to the child in private before each review. The *IRO Handbook* states that part of this pre-meeting is for the IRO to 'work with the child to discuss how s/he is likely to be able to make the most meaningful contribution' (DfES, 2010, p 20). Realistically, to make the meeting between the young person and the IRO meaningful it would need to take place at least a week prior to the review meeting. The *Handbook* goes on to state that a formal pre-meeting may not always be necessary and in such cases the IRO could 'simply make phone contact' to establish the child's wishes about the upcoming review (DfES, 2010, p 20), though the implication is that this would be the exception rather than the rule. However, having spoken to IROs in this study, it transpired that the reverse was true; in practice, IROs said that meeting children and young people between reviews only took place in rare circumstances. Unsurprisingly, the IROs viewed this as a barrier to children's and young people's meaningful participation (see Chapter 5). The lack of regular contact with their IRO was clearly evidenced during the interviews with young people: all ten reported that they never met with their IRO between review meetings. The following interaction with Mason, for example, was typical:

Clive:	Did you ever meet the IRO between reviews?
Mason:	What do you mean between?
Clive:	Did you ever meet them in between reviews, apart from that 10 or 15 minutes before?
Mason:	No.

Emma, when asked, said that she hadn't seen her IRO between review meetings:

Emma: She was really nice. She was a lovely woman. It's just a shame though because I would have liked to see her outside my reviews and stuff to have a catch-up or a chat because she was really down to earth, but I never had a proper like meet with her before the review.

Clive: Did you get the impression that that was because she was busy or she had lots on?

Emma: Maybe. I didn't really think about it. It was more of a kind of like – I saw that was her job and I genuinely thought that was the only reason she was there is to be in the meeting.

This exchange is particularly telling, as it shows that Emma's conception of her IRO's role is directed by the degree – or lack thereof – of exposure she had to her. Emma clearly would have welcomed the opportunity to build up more of a relationship with her IRO in the way stipulated in the *IRO Handbook*, but in reality she only got to meet with her at her review meeting and this therefore dictated the role that she thought the IRO held – merely to chair the meeting. Her experience therefore runs contrary to the notion of the IRO providing oversight of the case and helping her to provide her views on the care plan (as set out in the DfES, 2010). Despite her limited amount of interaction with her IRO, however, Emma did still hold positive view of her. This accords with the findings from our research in Local Authority One, in which we found that even though young people thought the IRO role was solely focused on chairing their review meeting they still had a positive view of them.

A number of previous studies (Munro, 2001; Bell, 2002; McLeod, 2006; Barnes, 2012; Jelicic et al, 2014) have concluded that a positive relationship between the young person and the SW and/or the IRO plays a key role in improving young people's participation in decision-making meetings. As Jelicic et al (2014, p 39) found, 'a good relationship with the IROs was crucial in children's understanding of their role in the care planning process, and this was mostly explained in terms of attitudes and ability to ensure the child's views are taken into consideration'. Similarly, for Roesch-Marsh et al (2016, p 907) 'relationships were found to be important at every stage of the review cycle including: preparation for the review, the review meeting itself, debriefing from the review and implementing plans'. While the high turnover of SWs in LAs continues to persist, IRO positions have remained comparatively stable. An obvious solution therefore would be for IROs to build on the support and consistency that they can provide to children and young people, for example, by visiting them between reviews. However, to do this IROs would have to have reasonable caseloads, which was not the case in the LAs where my research was carried out. In both authorities caseloads for IROs were significantly higher than the 50–70 caseload recommended by the *IRO Handbook*.

Young people's views of SWs

The personal attributes of SWs and IROs – such as listening skills – are a deciding factor in whether a meaningful relationship can be developed (McLeod, 2006). According to Pert et al (2014, p 5):

> Some children reported having a positive relationship with their social workers. Where children felt that they got to know their social worker as a 'real person' and not just a professional, they felt much more positive about them and the social work team generally ... those children who reported having positive relationships with their social worker also reported less negative feelings about their review process.

Pert et al's 2014 study considered young people's perceptions of reviews, while a similar study conducted by Muench et al (2017) explored young people's participation and engagement in Child Protection Conferences. Both studies concluded that where young people had a better relationship with their SW, they tended to be more positive about the meetings and LA input. Most of the young people I interviewed for this study reported having had at least one positive relationship with a SW during their time care. For example, Katy acknowledged that she was very challenging towards her SWs and she struggled to build relationships with many of them, but that there was one who 'went the extra mile' and this made all the difference.

> 'I gave her so much abuse but she'd just sit there and tap her fingers on the table or desk or anything. She wouldn't show ... she wouldn't flinch, she wouldn't do anything.

Does that make sense? … She was a bit … she was like so hard as a stone. I could never get through to her. But, do you know what, I ended up sticking to the routine of being in by four every day. I ended up getting into a routine and having boundaries. And I've learned from it now that actually her standing there doing nothing, not reacting, actually helped. I could be standing there frothing at the mouth going mad and she just didn't care. … But the point is she cared enough not to react, if that makes sense. … And because of that I do … I did quite like B; we got on after a while. … I ended up sending her some flowers when I realised how nice she was [laughs].'

Katy was clear that she had not trusted any of her previous SWs; in fact she had struggled to trust anyone in her life. Her SW's tactic (as Katy conceived of it) of 'caring enough not to react' – being calm and giving Katy the space to express herself – allowed her to gain Katy's trust. This very powerful interaction shows the significant impact that a 'good' SW can have on young people and how important it is that SWs are given the time to build up a meaningful relationship with their charge. Katy's positive relationship with this SW saw her eventually 'getting into a routine and having boundaries', which was clearly a very significant positive change for her and had a long-term beneficial impact. Notably, Katy's experience with this SW took place over a period of time: Katy tested the relationship and then saw that the response was consistent. The importance of taking time to build a meaningful relationship and adopting a consistent approach is plain to see.

Some of the other participants in this study expressed less-positive attitudes towards SWs. For example, Josh said:

'I don't like social workers, they really annoy me, coz they … um … ask the same questions all the time, [like] "do you feel happier", "do you like school".'

A commonly held view among the respondents was that some of their SWs had been incompetent or had failed to get anything done; indeed, all ten participants expressed to have had SWs at some point whom they had found unhelpful or who had not kept their promises.

One of this study's key findings was that when a young person reported having a poor relationship with their SW, they also tended to hold negative views on the CiC review meeting itself.

Kiera: [At the end of the meeting] I kind of felt … like a burden was lifted because it was tense. When I was in the meeting it was like tensed up and stuff like that because obviously I didn't build a relationship with my social worker. He was really bad, like he didn't do anything. He was so laid back that he didn't get anything done.

… he'd say all this stuff and he barely ever saw me as well. That's the main reason why I didn't really get to build a relationship. And then when he did see me he tried being like a buddy and it's just kind of like whoa – you never see me so you don't have the right to come and you haven't seen me like after God knows how many months and then act all pally-pally with me. Yeah so it was awkward … in the review because it was as if he knew me and I was like "well you don't", and with the IRO, it would not be a relationship outside the review and my foster carers were the only people in the room that I had a relationship with, but they weren't there to discuss my future and stuff … and my foster carers would give their view and their opinions and stuff like that but when the meeting ended it was like 'well thank God for that' kind of thing, so yeah, I just wanted to get on with my night.

If you have a good relationship with your social worker it works a little bit more because it's less of a meeting and more of a chat … it's an actual discussion instead of point to point things.

Clive: You said 'less of a meeting and more of a chat' …?

Kiera: Yes, if you have a relationship 'cos … if your social worker doesn't build a relationship with you it's just another person in the room and … it's uncomfortable and it's awkward.

This exchange highlights the impact Kiera's poor relationship with her SW had on her capacity to engage in the review meeting. Furthermore, in showing that her first thought when the meeting ended was 'thank God for that' (as it meant that she could 'get on with her night'), Kiera expressed a viewpoint which was echoed by many of the young people: that meetings are perceived to be a chore. Kiera also contrasted what a meeting with a SW that she got on with was like ('less of a meeting and more of a chat') against a meeting with a SW whom she did not have a positive relationship with (seemingly bureaucratic, entailing purely 'point to point things').

Kiera's views should be regarded in the context of the issues around SW retention and rapport building with young people, which were raised earlier on in this chapter. Guaranteeing the consistent presence of a professional in the life of a child or young person and thus enabling that professional to build a positive relationship with that child or young person are the essential foundations for participation and engagement. If, as some participants in this study reported, the SW doesn't see the young person very often and therefore is unable to build a relationship with them, they can come to be regarded as 'just another person in the room'. Kiera noted that her foster carer had, until recently, been the only person known to her at the review meetings – a set-up which would inevitably impact on her capacity to engage in her review. Again, the quality of the relationship between the IRO, SW and young person is seen to be a key determining factor in their engagement in the review process.

Some of the young participants reported having had positive relationships with at least one of their SWs. The knock-on effect on their level of engagement in the review process was marked. The interview with Charmaine exemplifies this clearly:

Clive: What about your good social worker?
Charmaine: Yeah, the one I had before now, I loved her to bits. She was just on it all the time and just on the ball. I didn't have to get on her case or anything. She just had everything done and ...
Clive: What sorts of things?
Charmaine: Even when she didn't agree with what I wanted she'd still do it anyway. ... So my first foster placement, it broke down just after I was 16 and I said to her I really didn't wanna go to another foster placement, I wanted to go to supported housing or something like that and she was like, 'No, no. I don't want you to do it.' She still took it to her manager anyway. She still fought my case as much as she could. But obviously they said no because I'd literally just turned 16. But she managed to get me part-time in a training flat. So that was really good of her 'cos even though she was really against

> it herself she still did everything she could. ...
> [A] lot of social workers would have just not even
> bothered and then said, 'Oh no, they said no.'

This interaction with Charmaine is typical of other interviews and demonstrates that young people will form a judgement of their SW based at least in part on their perceived level of competency and ability to keep to their promises. What came through very strongly in all of the interviews conducted for this study was that if a young person had a positive relationship with their SW and had trust and faith in them to 'get things done', they would be much more likely to engage with the review process and decision making more generally. The quality of the young person–SW relationship is therefore of crucial importance, since the effectiveness of the review process and the young person's level of engagement more broadly turns on this relationship and, specifically, the individual skills and ability of the SW. However, even when professionals have forged good relationships with young people the review process itself can still be problematic, as the next section will demonstrate.

Young people's perceptions of the review meetings

There has been limited research to date into children's and young people's views of reviews. As discussed in Chapter 2, some 20 years ago Thomas and O'Kane (1999) interviewed young people about their views of reviews and they concluded that they found the meetings 'scary' and 'boring'. This study was carried out before the introduction of the IRO role.

In order to find out the extent of the role played by children and young people in their review meetings, I put to all of the participants in this study a series of questions:

1. Did they choose when the meeting was going to take place?
2. Did they choose where the meeting was going to be held?
3. Did they decide what was on the agenda?
4. Did they decide who was going to be invited?

By ensuring that the interviews covered these four essential components, I was then able to compare the participants' answers to the answers given by the IROs and SWs to questions on a similar theme.

Apart from three participants who had chaired their own reviews, the majority of participants said that they had played no role in choosing when their review took place, where it was held, who was invited or what was on the agenda. This was echoed by the SWs and IROs who were interviewed as part of this study (see Chapter 5). Having little or no involvement in the decision making around such key elements of the meeting will necessarily have limited the ability of the children and young people to participate meaningfully in the process. If we consider this evidence in the context of Hart's (1992) ladder of participation, we might reasonably conclude that the young people's participation in their reviews was tokenistic.

Of the ten young people interviewed for this study, eight said that they found their reviews to be both frustrating and stressful. For example, Kiera gave the following account:

> '[My reviews were] a little bit frustrating because there were certain things in my case that couldn't be helped. Like I would want more contact with my brother and sister, but ... they were going through adoption and fostering and everything else, and they ... didn't think it was appropriate. Obviously that made me very upset. So my reviews were a bit of a whirlwind, if that makes sense ... there would be meltdown moments, but it would be because of certain things, but most of it would get sorted. ... Like, all my health checks would be sorted ... the day-to-day schooling would be sorted, all of that stuff, but when it came to contact ... the IRO would help me try and get it but it's obviously not her decision, that's up to the social worker.'

Although reviews can be very stressful, as the interview with Kiera attests, the feedback from this study shows that they have the capacity to be effective at resolving fairly straightforward matters such as ensuring young people are seeing a dentist regularly. However, their efficacy seems to decline when it comes to finding solutions to more complex issues, such as enabling contact with siblings that have been placed for adoption.

A small number of the young people interviewed in this study had had very negative experiences of reviews. For example, Katy highlighted a whole host of issues she had experienced, including the presence of 'strangers' at her review meeting, which had meant that both her experience of the meeting itself and how she felt about it afterwards were far from positive.

Katy: Most kids haven't got a clue what's going on ... I feel like they tried to tell me in the early days [what the purpose of the review was] but I just didn't want to listen to them because I hated everybody. If someone had sat me down, fed me some pizza, ... chilled for a bit and then started talking about some serious stuff I might have accepted it.

It was the fact that it was just thrown on top of me, 'hey, here's a meeting', for the first one, 'go talk about all your problems' basically is what it felt to me, and then you feel judged by everyone around you. Because the first meeting you might have [the] police there. ... I had police for the very first meeting, I had loads of people, and I didn't know who half of them were. ... But that meeting I had no choice to attend. I was kind of picked up by the social worker and dragged there and then returned to the foster home ...

Clive: You were literally dragged to the meeting?

Katy: Pretty much [laughs].

Clive: How did you feel generally at the end of the meetings?

Katy: Sometimes emotionally and physically drained. If something had been agreed that was going to go forward that was good, like letterbox contact or something, then I could be ecstatic. But I would say a good six out of ten times I would come away from it crying my eyes out.

Katy's powerful testimony highlights a number of crucial points. Firstly, young people should always have the choice not to attend their review meetings; it should be their decision to make. The notion that Katy was practically 'dragged' to her review against her will is extremely concerning. Furthermore, young people should have the choice as to who attends their review; not knowing and therefore not feeling at ease with the other participants is an obvious barrier to feeling engaged and that they are being 'heard' in the review meeting, and could even be construed as oppressive practice. Eight of the interviewees said that they would have preferred if fewer people had attended their reviews; this accords with our research in Local Authority One, which also concluded that the number of professionals attending reviews acts as a barrier to participation and engagement. Likewise, Katy's experience of her first meeting as being particularly challenging resonates with findings in earlier research (Roesch-Marsh et al, 2016).

Of the ten participants, six had mixed feelings or slightly negative views of their review meetings. Of the four young people who reported positive views of their review meetings, three had chaired their own meetings. From the six who had negative or ambivalent views of their reviews, George's experience neatly summarises certain aspects of their experiences:

Clive: So how did you find the meetings generally?

George: I don't know. I was a quiet kid so I just sat there and like, nodded along and it felt like because I did that they didn't really engage with me properly and they were talking around me instead of to me. So they basically had ... a mindset of 'Well he's not engaging so we shouldn't engage with him'.

Clive: And how did that make you feel?

George: A little bit peeved. ... I was a bit annoyed most of the time but I got to a point where I was just like 'Okay, so this is like the norm' so I just didn't really care by that point.

The impression we get from this exchange is that the process has made George even more vulnerable than he was already. Decisions are made over so many parts of George's life which he had demonstrably little control over, and it is difficult to see that this extends to the way in which his review – a process which should have him at its heart – is conducted. These feelings of ambivalence, resignation or hopelessness in relation to the sense of control George expressed about his review were shared by the other children and young people interviewed in this study. This finding has also been drawn out by earlier studies (Thomas and O'Kane, 1999; Munro, 2001; Roesch-Marsh et al, 2016).

The interviewees in this study volunteered various suggestions as to what could have been done to enable them participate more meaningfully in their reviews. Ultimately, if they were able to feel more comfortable and relaxed in the meeting, they would be more likely to engage. For each young person, this meant slightly different things. Kiera, for example, felt that being allowed to bring a friend to her first review would have helped:

Clive: Would you like your friends there?

Kiera: At one point I think I would have. When I first went into care if I knew I had the option to I probably would have brought in my best friend who I had known for a while to be there with me, because he'd known and still does know everything like that's going on. So if I'd known that was an option I probably would have dragged him along at the start. It would have made me feel a little bit more comfortable.

I didn't realise you could have your friends there until a couple of weeks ago actually. You get to choose whoever's there like anyone you want to make you obviously feel like more at ease because it's your review.

For a young person who lacks an established or positive relationship with their designated team of professionals, being allowed to bring a friend or close family member might make all the difference. Another way of feeling comfortable and relaxed – in any setting – is to feel that you are in control, which possibly explains the success of those review meetings which the children and young people in question were allowed to chair themselves and/or set the agenda for the meeting.

The importance of young people being actively involved throughout the review process, including in agenda setting, has previously been identified by Roesch-Marsh et al (2016). For the seven participants in this study who did not chair their reviews, had no role in agenda setting for their review or indeed in the process of deciding who attended the meeting, when it took place or where it took place, participation can be regarded as merely tokenistic (Hart, 1992).

Katy, who chaired her own review meeting, raised in her interview the subject of agenda setting and the tension between the things that she wanted to discuss and those that the professionals 'needed' to discuss:

Clive: So there were certain things that had to be discussed?

Katy: Yeah, obviously. Those were the things that were on the list. ... So, like those things we discussed normally at the end. The things I didn't like would be discussed at the end. So, we discussed about all the good things, like school, home, contact with my dad, all of those type of things. And then it would come to the bad things like substance misuse

Clive:
Katy:

and … sex exploitation and all those type of things. So like … things I didn't want to talk about but had no choice in it [laughs].

Clive: Do you feel like you didn't have any choice?

Katy: Well, no, it's the fact that they'd kind of talk about it if I wasn't there anyway. … So, I would rather be there and be like 'I can sit here and fight my battle' than walk away and be called guilty for something I haven't done.

This exchange exemplifies the disconnect between the 'good' things which Katy wanted to discuss at her review and the 'bad' things which she felt forced to discuss. These 'bad' things are no doubt issues of great concern to professionals who play a role in the care and protection of vulnerable children and young people, hence why they form discussion points in meetings such as reviews. However, for the young person whose review it is, discussing these issues is uncomfortable: they might feel that either they are not relevant to them or that they are not things that it is their role to be concerned about. It is noteworthy that Katy still wanted to be there for the part of the meeting in which these things were discussed so that she could 'fight [her] battle'. For those young people who lack the same confidence shown by Katy to chair their review meeting and assist in setting the agenda, there is a real risk that the requirement to discuss issues such as child sexual exploitation could lead to them further disengaging from the process.

Katy's stance appears to be a combative one: she typifies the discussion of 'bad' things in her review as a 'battle' which she must 'fight'. Although Katy was involved in the review process and – according to Hart's (1992) ladder of participation – deemed to be 'engaged', this engagement is qualified and fuelled, in part, by a desire not to be misunderstood or blamed. This point will be discussed further in the following chapter when we discuss professionals' views of review meetings.

In contrast to the previous literature in this area, some of the participants who were interviewed as part of this study displayed a much more positive view of their review meetings. Tellingly, this appears to be explained by the fact that they chaired their own reviews. While only three of the ten participants chaired their own meetings, all of these were positive about the meetings and the review process more generally. Charmaine was one of these:

Charmaine: [Review meetings are] alright. I chair them.

Clive:	So tell me about the last review you had, or one of the last reviews you had. How did it work?
Charmaine:	I go there, then me and [the IRO] go in the room first and we talk. Then everyone else gets invited into the room, then we just talk about everything we talk about.
Clive:	So do you agree the agenda, what you're going to talk about, with [the IRO]?
Charmaine:	Yes.

Emma, another young person who chaired her own review, said:

'I don't understand why people wouldn't want to chair it, in my perspective, because it's a bunch of people in a room talking about you.'

This is an interesting point: it seems that Emma decided to chair the meeting in part so as to regain some level of control over the process. She clearly understood that it was a meeting about her and that therefore it was essential that she played a central role in it, including by acting as chair. Emma came across as assertive and self-confident and expressed clear views about what she wanted from her reviews. Not all young people are as confident – George is one such example – and for these individuals the concern is that even if they were offered the opportunity to chair the meeting, they would choose not to as they would feel they lacked the confidence to do so.

Chloe was also positive about the experience of chairing her own review:

Clive:	Has that been a positive experience?
Chloe:	Yeah. For the first time I did it we sort of, like, did it together and then now I just do it on my own.

As yet, there has not been any research into the experience of young people chairing their own reviews and analysis of the impact this has on their ability to participate meaningfully in the review process. It is clear from this study however that enabling young people to chair their reviews is highly empowering for them and engenders greater participation in the process and in decision making more generally. In the LAs where this research was carried out, around 100 children at any given time chair their own reviews. Chapter 5 looks more in depth at professionals' views of this phenomenon. Looking at this through the prism of Hart's ladder of participation, it could be argued that children chairing their own reviews is at least rung 6 (adults initiate and share decisions with children) and potentially even rung 8 (children and adults share decision making). By contrast, young people who did not chair their meetings were more likely to be on rung 3 (tokenistic). However, it is important to be aware of the limitations to Hart's (1992) ladder; for example, Thomas (2000, p 174) argues that a 'ladder' is too 'linear to encompass the multidimensional character of children's participation about their lives'. He goes on to emphasise the complexity of participation in a review meeting and suggests that we need to consider not just how much a child says in a meeting but also how much notice is taken of what they say by other participants and how well the young person understands the issues that are being discussed. The next chapter will consider the professionals' perspectives on these issues.

Summary

This chapter raised a number of points which will be considered further in the chapters that follow. What comes through very clearly in the interviews with children and young people is that although they had experienced numerous different SWs, there had been at least one SW with whom they had built up a positive working relationship. These findings, in terms of what young people wanted from their SWs and what aided their engagement, was largely in line with the findings from previous studies (Thomas, 2002; McLeod, 2006); that is, they wanted a SW who listened to them, was reliable and who did what they said they were going to do. It was disheartening to find through this study that although most of the young people who were interviewed had a positive relationship with their IRO, they did not see them between reviews and most were not even aware that this was a possibility, let alone something which is actively promoted by the *IRO Handbook* (DfES, 2010).

This research also found that those young people who chaired their own reviews felt more meaningfully engaged in the review process and had the opportunity to have their 'say' or voice heard in respect of key aspects of the plans for the meeting, such as when and where the review took place, who was invited and what was on the agenda. The concept of children and young people chairing their own reviews is still fairly new and it is positive that this research (despite its small sample size) demonstrates its capacity to work well in practice and facilitate meaningful participation.

The following chapter will draw out the points raised by the children and young people in relation to professionals' accounts. It will explore SWs' and IROs' views on participation and relationship building and discuss why IROs do not meet with children and young people between reviews. It will also examine the thoughts of these professionals on the practice of children and young people chairing their own reviews, along with the level of control over the agenda and decision making that they feel could or should be provided to children and young people during this process.

5

Young people's participation: views from social workers and independent reviewing officers

Introduction

In the previous chapter I explored children's and young people's views of CiC reviews and discussed the barriers that they felt affected their participation. I then went on to discuss what children and young people felt could help them to participate more meaningfully in their review meetings. This chapter builds on that foundational base by considering data drawn from the eight interviews with IROs and eleven interviews with SWs regarding young peoples' participation in reviews and more broadly about decisions that were made about their lives. It will examine whether similar themes emerge from the IROs' and SWs' perspectives or whether their views differ from those held by the children and young people.

During my analysis, I identified a number of themes and – when the data were further refined – a number of further sub-themes. Sub-themes 'can be useful for giving structure to a particularly large and complex theme, and also for demonstrating the hierarchy of meaning within the data' (Braun and Clarke, 2006, p 84). The themes and sub-themes identified were as follows:

1. Barriers to effective participation:
   a) SWs' and IROs' high caseloads and ensuing time pressures;
   b) the high turnover of SWs and inexperienced staff;
   c) lack of understanding and training of professionals in 'participation';
   d) children's and young people's negative experiences in reviews and ensuing reticence about attending;
   e) balancing parents' rights and child's needs;
   f) structure and focus of the review not being child-centred.
2. Factors which assist participation:
   a) quality of the relationship between the child and the professionals;

b) the child/young person chairing their own review meeting.

These key themes and sub-themes will be explored in relation to the interview data and their correspondence with previous research.

Barriers to effective participation

A common theme that emerged during the interviews with the IROs and SWs – and to an extent with the young participants also – was the feeling that IROs and SWs were under a great deal of pressure and that they were struggling to carry out their role in the manner that they would wish to, or indeed as statutory guidance such as the *IRO Handbook* (DfES, 2010) determines that they should. 'Barriers to effective participation' covered a range of different aspects in the working life and practices of IROs and SWs and they will be considered in turn in the following sections.

High caseloads and time pressures on both SWs and IROs

All the SWs and IROs interviewed as part of this study indicated that they were under a great deal of pressure and struggling to fulfil the requirements of their role as stipulated in statutory guidance. High caseloads were a particular challenge highlighted by all the IROs and SWs. The following interaction illustrates the challenge posed to participation of children in CiC review meetings when IRO caseloads are high:

> 'We've got so many kids coming into care, they're trying to manage going out and seeing children in between reviews – it's really difficult. So it tends to be maybe picking them up half an hour beforehand and if you've got a complex case or a complex child it needs that additional support, trying to do something in half an hour is a bit more difficult. It's not impossible once you've built a relationship up – then, half an hour is fine. ... I don't want to sound like it's not that they don't go well – but for me, any Child in Care Review, you wing it and if you don't wing it – I know that's awful to say – but you manage what you get delivered. That's what social work is about. You know, you deal with crises don't you. ... But for me that's what social work is about and because my background has always been front line, for me as long as I get to the end of the meeting and I get things

covered then I've done my job. Whether I've been sworn
at a bit in the process, so be it [laughs].' (IRO 3)

This suggests that even the review process – which should be carefully
planned – has instead become another crisis meeting. A plethora of
research has evidenced that frontline duty work can be very challenging
due to the difficulty of planning for every eventuality (Munro, 2012;
Bowyer and Roe, 2015; Shoesmith, 2016). However, IRO 3 suggests
that IROs are routinely unprepared for review meetings and see the
meetings as 'crises' and something they need to 'deal with'. IRO 3's
description of 'winging it' was fairly consistent with the way other
IROs and SWs described the meetings. This 'crisis' culture would
certainly present a challenge to the ability of children and young
people to actively engage in the review process.

All the SWs and IROs went on to link the detrimental impact high
caseloads had upon their ability to ensure that the child or young
person was able to participate in their review in a meaningful manner,
a point which was also raised by many of the young people. The
implication is that children and young people feel, at times, that their
allocated professionals do not have time for them.

Most of the IROs interviewed in this study commented that they
needed to spend time in reviews challenging poor practice by SWs
and that this could detract from their ability to ensure that children
participated meaningfully in their meetings. This requirement to
challenge the SW – in front of the child or young person – is likely
to have an impact on how the child subsequently engages with the
review process. The child or young person may feel let down by the
SW and that they are not doing their job properly, and there could be
an ensuing impact on how or whether they choose to engage.

This commonly accepted reality of having too much work relates
closely to the culture of the profession (Shoesmith, 2016; Muench
et al, 2017; Leigh, 2017). This issue was clearly articulated by IRO 3:

Clive: Do you think SWs have the time and resources to
           prepare people for the meetings?
IRO 3:   No. But I think they could make time and find
           time to some degree. I think that stat visits[1] aren't
           often done, so if they were doing their stat visits
           more regularly those ... could be part of preparing
           children. It's about making use of the time they do
           have. They're so busy ... they're so, so, busy, and I
           don't mean just on the ground but in their heads.

> They've got so many things they're carrying, so many pressures … they're not able to think ahead or plan ahead because everything is on the ground.

This notion of being 'busy' resonates with research carried out by Ruch (2012), which identifies the problem of SWs being busy and having no time to think, plan or feel. Forrester (2016) calls this 'zombie social work'; reflecting on the challenges of modern-day child protection social work, he contends:

> In research we frequently observe SWs doing a visit because they are meant to do one within a certain timescale (the "stat visit"). Their computer is literally flashing at them, they do the visit, fill in the form and the computer stops flashing. But the visit itself is often characterised by a purposelessness that leaves worker and family confused about what is happening. … To me this is symptomatic of a system which has developed an obsession with effective management, without sufficient attention to the wider values and aims of the service. It is like a zombie social work – moving and busy (very, very busy!) without any sense of being truly alive. (Forrester, 2016, p 12)

Forrester's comments accord well with the view of social work depicted in my research: of an inexperienced, transient workforce which is so busy filling out forms that they afford little thought or consideration as to how children or their parents are involved in their practice generally and specifically in decision making and review meetings; teachers and foster carers using review meetings as a means to criticise young people; and tokenistic (at best) participation by young people where they play no role in making key decisions surrounding their care.

Overall, these research findings lead to the unfortunate conclusion that the Munro Review (2012) had very little impact on the way the child protection system works. It appears we still have a system premised upon 'doing things right rather than doing the right thing' (Munro, 2012). The following quote from Ruch et al (2008) about a SW who had moved to England from abroad to work in a child protection team in 2008 is still very relevant today and these views are certainly borne out in my research:

> I am working in a factory. … We produce initial and core assessments in our factory. Our management counts the

assessments completed on a weekly basis and informs the workers of the results in team meetings and by email. The workers don't seem to care about these numbers but they preoccupy the management. There have been many changes in our factory in the past five years. The management has been replaced, the teams were reconstructed, the machinery (workers, forms, IT systems) also saw great changes.

The management measures (in percentages) the reports of initial and core assessments completed on time, and compare these to other teams. When the team manager reports these statistics in team meetings, I can recognise how my body becomes tense and my heart rate increases, and I get very angry.....I have voiced my resentment to this ritual, but it was ignored by managers and other colleagues. (Ruch et al, 2008, p 89)

A number of useful parallels can be drawn between this quote, Forrester's observations about so-called zombie SWs and the comments made by participants in my study. The IROs acknowledged that reviews took place without young people attending as the meeting had to occur within a certain timeframe. This meant that the young people did not always actually attend the review as it did not fit with the IRO's or SW's diary. The interview with IRO 3 illustrates how this can happen:

Clive:	If you could change anything about Child in Care Reviews to increase participation, what would it be?
IRO 3:	Demand ... I think it's ultimately about time. If there were more time to prepare then IROs would insist on children being present, because you'd have the time to help prepare for that and to meet those around, and SWs would have the time to prepare ... and plan for it.
Clive:	Do reviews ever take place where children just wouldn't be able to attend because of your diary and the social worker's diary, and there's no way they could attend?
IRO 3:	Yeah. Sadly, yes. ... Because they're in school and you can't fit it in anywhere else; because you can't get everybody together. Although, we do have the option of two-part reviews. They're not the nicest reviews to hold as an IRO because they become complicated ... you miss information and you

repeat information so they get a bit muddly, so we try and avoid them.

In their interviews, both the IROs and the SWs documented numerous incidents of meetings taking place to meet arbitrary timescales – a practice which Munro (2012) is highly critical of. It appears common in this LA for review meetings to take place without children and young people even being aware that they are happening, because professionals are under pressure to ensure they occur within a certain set timeframe. Review meetings are required to take place within thirty days of a change of placement, at three months and then every six months thereafter. One IRO raised the example of a review meeting (to which the young person was invited) taking place on the child's birthday so as to meet the statutory timescale. Arguably, this is symptomatic of a system that, due to its narrow focus on meeting targets and timescales, has forgotten that young people are (or should be) at the heart of everything we do – truly, 'zombie social work' (Forrester, 2016) in practice. Applying Hart's (1992) ladder of participation, this practice could rightfully be placed into the category of the bottom rung – 'manipulation'.

As a time-saving measure, a number of SWs reported that they would combine CiC reviews with PEP meetings at the school of the child or young person in question. SW 1 recalled having back-to-back meetings comprising a PEP meeting at the school with just the professionals, which was then followed by the CiC review meeting involving the child.

Clive: Did that seem to work well?
SW 1:   Quite well. I suppose, as long as there's not the repetition of it. It just means they can end up being quite long meetings and a child might be more comfortable if it is in their home instead of being dragged out of class, sit round with however many professionals looking at them and then leave again. But I think it depends. ... I have one boy that very much just thought it was a process and he'd sit there like 'great, I've just got to do this'.

This description of a young person being 'dragged out of class [to] sit round with however many professionals looking at them and then leave again' accords with the experience of a young person (Katy) in Chapter 4, in which she describes being 'dragged' to her review.

SW 1 is clearly not carrying out high-quality child-focused practice by holding the CiC review and the PEP meeting at the same time; it is patently a time-saving measure, and one can see from the sarcastic response of the young person referred to by SW 1 that it is likely to hinder their participation in the meeting. This would appear to be further evidence of a beleaguered workforce who are under a great deal of pressure and do not have the time or knowledge to carry out basic social work practice (Tickle, 2018). Mannay et al (2017) also found that on occasion children in care are taken out of education by SWs, which has the potential to impact negatively on their educational attainment.

All the IROs asserted that it was up to the SW to prepare the young person for the review and then it was the responsibility of the IRO to check at the meeting that this had been done properly. IROs also considered that part of this preparation work was filling out the consultation form with the child and that though this bureaucratic process was important the child's participation was effectively minimal. Both the young people interviewed for the research and the young people we interviewed in Local Authority One were vocal in their criticism of the use of consultation forms. However, the importance of the forms to the IROs is outlined in the following interaction with IRO 4:

IRO 4:   The social worker definitely needs to talk with them and ensure that the consultation paper is filled out at least and talk about how the review's going to work for them. ... That often doesn't happen though − their foster carer or residential worker and ideally the parents too if they are having good regular contact might have a chat too.

Clive: Do you think SWs and IROs have the time and resources to prepare young people properly for the meetings?

IRO 4:   Not always, no. As a part-time IRO I think my caseload was fifty-something so it's impossible to do that −

Clive: Is that three days a week?

IRO 4:   Yes, it's impossible on every single case to do so you had to choose those cases you were most worried about and make sure that you dedicate time to those, and the same with SWs. But the problem is those stable long-term placements, those children get a rough deal 'cos they're the ones that the social worker and the IRO often don't … have the time to go out and visit before – I mean the guidance is clear that ideally we should be going out, but you couldn't do that. … I always aspired to that as an IRO, that it wouldn't just be about I'd see them ten, fifteen minutes before reviews, I really wanted to have got to a point where I visited young people in between reviews but I only ever managed to get to that when I was in dispute with the Local Authority.

This quote highlights the fact that the only occasion in which this particular IRO managed to uphold her statutory duty (that is, visiting children between reviews, as stipulated by the *IRO Handbook* [DfES, 2010]) was when she was in a dispute with the LA. Since this is a very rare scenario in this LA and most others, the inference we can draw is that only a very small proportion of children are visited between reviews. IRO 4 also raises the point that it is potentially up to the parent to play a role in preparing young people for review meetings, but whether parents understand the review process, and whether it is appropriate to expect a parent to prepare a young person for a review meeting, is questionable.

While one would expect that parents may not understand the review process, more worrying was the suggestion by some IROs that in their view SWs sometimes struggled to prepare children and young people for reviews as they were lacking in experience and did not understand the review process themselves sufficiently. The focus on filling out forms and the imbalance between direct work and administrative tasks has been highlighted in previous studies (Holmes and McDermid, 2013; BASW, 2018) and again is an issue which my research has highlighted. The impact of inexperienced professionals upon meaningful participation is explored further in the following section, along with the impact of a high turnover of staff.

High turnover and inexperienced SWs

Almost all the SWs and IROs interviewed as part of this study raised the high turnover of SWs as a potential barrier to participation by young people. The following interview extract illustrates how the issue of a high turnover of staff and an inexperienced workforce in this LA was impacting on the way that children and young people were prepared for reviews. This was presented as being partly due to the SWs themselves not understanding the purpose of the review.

Clive: Whose responsibility do you think it is to prepare children and young people for reviews?

IRO 3:   Social workers. ... Part of my role, I believe, is to help support that. ... I think the challenge is though, a lot of social workers don't really know what to expect from a Child in Care Review. Not all, but obviously you've got a lot of newly qualified social workers coming through and we have a lot of turnover of staff in terms of training. So often the social worker comes to a review and they might not know what to expect so aren't really able to prepare the child, which makes it very difficult then.

Clive: Because the social worker doesn't know themselves what it means now?

IRO 3:   Potentially, yeah. And also we all practice slightly differently so I think there's an issue about IROs being consistent because we're independent and not really managed by anybody, although we have a team manager. They're there to guide us rather than manage us, so we kind of march to our own drums to a degree and then we have very clear legislation to back us up. We all do things slightly differently.

This quote raises two issues: inconsistencies within the IRO team regarding the way that different IROs manage the review meeting and the possibility that inexperienced SWs do not themselves understand the purpose of reviews. This was also evidenced in my interview with IRO 7:

'They [SWs] should be talking with them and asking questions like, 'what's the best venue for you?' 'These were the things that we talked about last time; what's been going well?' 'What are some of the things you might want to talk about?' That, in my experience, often doesn't happen and so I've been at reviews, sadly, where young people don't know what the plan's going to be, let alone think about things that we need to talk about, so that can make it really, really difficult to have an honest and open discussion.' (IRO 7)

The point IRO 7 is making is that, since the SW has not explained to the young person the plan, and in some cases may not even be clear what the plan is, a barrier automatically exists which prevents the meeting from fulfilling one of its core roles – to review the care plan (DfES, 2010). This will clearly impact on the opportunity for the young person to engage in the review meeting, as – like IRO 7 and many other IROs reported – the review turns into a meeting to outline what the care plan is, instead of this having been carried out prior to the review and involving the young person, parents and foster carers. This echoes IRO 3's view at the beginning of this chapter, of the meeting not being properly planned. Indeed, the basic function of the meeting is not to make the plan but to review the care plan (DfES, 2010; Dickens et al, 2015). If there is no plan in place and it has not been agreed with the child and parents, it is very difficult for the review meeting to review the plan and thus carry out its core function.

The importance of this in terms of working effectively alongside families was also emphasised by IRO 7:

IRO 7:	I've been at many a review where I've had to explain what twin-tracking[2] is and we've got a plan for twin-track, and that's not the purpose of the review, you know; that should have happened way before but –
Clive:	They don't know the plans (the parents)?
IRO 7:	No, nine times out of ten, you spend time at the end with the parents, thinking with them about what twin-tracking is. … If you've got a care plan it often hasn't been shared beforehand with parents. … I can probably think of quite a few reviews where I've asked the social worker to explain what the plan is in terms of twin-tracking and they've sort of said, can you do it?
Clive:	Why?
IRO 7:	Because I don't think they quite know – there's confusion around what we mean by twin-tracking still I think in the Local Authority.
Clive:	Is that because of lack of experience from the social work team?
IRO 7:	Yeah, yeah, maybe.

This point was also raised by a SM who stated in her interview that SWs were not drafting or updating care plans or reviewing plans at review meetings. This raises wider issues than just participation and suggests that SWs are not carrying out the basic legally required duties such as writing and updating care plans. Furthermore, it appears that SWs are not confident in explaining care plans to parents or children/ young people and that on occasion they are inappropriately delegating the responsibility of explaining the care plan at the review meeting to the IRO. This is not the IRO's role, nor is it the role of the meeting. Arguably then, this divergence from the core purpose of the meeting can be attributed in part to an inexperienced social work workforce which lacks confidence in its own decision making. This issue of inexperience and a lack of understanding will be examined in more detail in the following section, specifically in relation to the meaning of participation.

Lack of understanding and training of professionals in meaningful 'participation'

Although the IROs in this study, like the SWs, recognised how important participation is, most of the IROs were more aware than the SWs of the failings of the current system to ensure meaningful participation with children and young people. This could be because the IROs were more experienced social care professionals. It may also be because a central tenet of the IRO role is to ensure that all views are heard and considered.

Only one of the IROs had received any training on participation, and many reported that the training generally for IROs is very poor. For example, IRO 5 reported the following:

> 'I went on some BAAF (British Association of Adoption and Fostering) IRO training a few years ago in Manchester which covered stuff like that [participation] ... the training for IROs is atrocious, I have to say. ... We used to look as a team for training and find bits and pieces from BAAF or whoever and we'd go on it and we'd think, actually – not being arrogant – but we knew that.'

This quote reflects the wider experience of the IROs interviewed, of poor provision of IRO training generally and, specifically, a dearth of guidance on participation. Within this study of twenty-three professionals, only two – one SW and one SM – had ever attended training on participation.

All the SWs interviewed agreed that it was very important that children participate in their review meetings. However, there was confusion about what participation meant. SW 8 offered a definition of participation which was fairly typical of those offered by other SWs in the study:

> 'Participation to me just means a group of people all working together for the same goal or an achievement.' (SW 8)

Arguably, this definition more accurately describes inter-agency working and does not appear to relate to legal or theoretical definitions of children's participation. As outlined in the literature review, the most common model for considering child participation is Hart's (1992) ladder of participation. The ladder outlines the various types of participation from 'tokenism' to 'partnership', the latter describing a situation where children and the adults who are working with them possess equal amounts of influence and power over decisions made about the child's future (Bessell and Gal, 2009).

Hart (1992) acknowledges that the level of participation will differ depending upon the situation and the particular child. Nonetheless, for participation to be successful it is imperative that organisations are committed to genuine, rather than tokenistic, participation. When considering the interview data produced with IROs, children and young people, and SWs, in relation to Hart's ladder of participation, children's and young people's participation in reviews was most often presented as tokenistic at best, and often as manipulative.

One potential reason for SWs having such a poor understanding of what participation means is the fact that very few of them had ever attended training on participation. This suggests that in this LA, training on participation was not a priority, which led in this case to SWs and IROs possessing seemingly only a basic understanding of what participation means. Furthermore, this reality is likely to impact upon the ability of these professionals to practice in a manner which ensures children have an opportunity to participate in decisions that are made about their lives. This is in direct contravention to the UNCRC 1989 and the core social work values in relation to empowerment of service users (BASW, 2018).

There was also an observable disconnect between the importance placed on participation by SWs and the extent to which they actually tried to ensure that children participated in their meetings. Tellingly, while all eleven SWs said that children's participation in review meetings was very important, they also all stated that it was either they or the IRO who made the key decisions regarding the practicalities of the meeting. This disconnect appears to align with the findings of Argyris and Schön (1974), who found that people have aspirations and ideas that are developed through mental maps which comprise of theories of action. Argyris and Schön develop a distinction between 'espoused theory' (what people say) and 'theory in use' (what people actually do). 'Espoused theory' is defined as being:

> When someone is asked how he would behave in certain circumstances, the answer he usually gives is his espoused theory in action for that situation. This is the theory of action to which he gives allegiance and which, upon request, he communicates to others. (Argyris and Schön, 1974, p 7)

By contrast, 'theory in use' is defined as:

> [T]he theory which actually governs his actions is his theory in use, which may or may not be compatible with his espoused theory; furthermore, the individual may or may not be aware of this incompatibility. (Argyris and Schön, 1974, p 7)

When applying these concepts to this research, it was noted that the SWs articulated that while they view children's participation as being important, when it comes down to it their practice does not lead to children participating meaningfully. It is important to note that there is no suggestion of deception or deliberate manipulation by professionals in this situation; it is more the case that there is a dissonance between what is espoused and what actually takes place in practice.

All the SWs who were interviewed highlighted the importance of participation, while at the same time acknowledging that young people played no role in deciding key questions around review meeting logistics: when reviews took place, where they took place and who was invited. This is a clear example of espoused theory over theory in use.

Children's and young people's negative experiences in reviews and ensuing reticence about attending

The *IRO Handbook* states that the review meeting should be child-centred and, whenever possible, the young person should attend (DfES, 2010). However, it would not be appropriate to force a young person to attend a review meeting, and young people should be free to not attend and still have the opportunity to meet with the IRO separately, should they wish to.

Archard and Skivenes (2009, p 393) rightly state that 'children should not be intimidated by the circumstances in which they are asked to present their views'. It was concerning therefore that all the IROs reported other professionals (especially school staff and foster carers) using review meetings to blame and shame the young person. This is a worrying finding and it is noteworthy that similar research by Dickens et al (2015), Jelicic et al (2014) and Thomas and O'Kane (1999) previously has not highlighted this as an issue. The following interview extracts below demonstrate this problematic practice.

IRO 1: Foster carers and teachers will use the review as an opportunity to shame the child by bringing up their bad behaviour.

Clive: Have you got any examples of that?

IRO 1: I did a review at a secondary school the other day. The boy is in Year 7 [age group 11–12] with quite a few additional needs and his care plan is complex, but he was on that day facing permanent exclusion and the Head had made a decision that he couldn't enter the school that day for his review. That got turned around but then there were about four education representatives and ... the big male teacher, Head of Year, he wanted to take us through the whatever, 28 incidents, and he was a tiny little boy, very small for his age with some physical disability, and I could just see him shrivelling up. So how on earth can that child have a voice in that meeting if somebody just says 'oh, and on the 14th of the month you called your teacher an effing bitch' or whatever. You know, it's really unhelpful ... and foster carers sometimes will talk about behaviour incidents, I think sometimes to justify or to defend their own position.

It is clearly inappropriate to use the review as a mechanism to 'settle scores' with young people or to seek to shame them. The bullying behaviour IRO 1 described is not appropriate for a review meeting or indeed any other meeting and plainly should not be the way that professionals treat young people, regardless of the circumstances.

Overall, the IROs reported that this practice of being blamed, shamed or placed under the spotlight was a major barrier to children and young people attending their reviews, let alone engaging and participating in them. For example, this exchange with IRO 2 outlines how this pressure on the young person can reduce the chances of meaningful participation:

Clive: What do you think the main things are that lead to good participation from young people in children's care reviews?

IRO 2:   Well, I suppose they've got to feel safe. … [They] feel like they're under the spotlight. They're being kind of criticised, everyone's talking about them, everyone's looking at them, they're worried about bad things that will be said and so that's the kind of thing which deters young people.

Both of the quotes from IRO 1 and 2 outline how these meetings lead to young people feeling blamed, but they also provide an explanation for Katy's combative approach outlined in Chapter 4, here she detailed how she had to go to a review to 'fight her corner'. Although Mannay et al (2017) highlight that some teachers had oppressive views in relation to children in care, no previous research has outlined quite as clearly as this how stressful, difficult and oppressive a review meeting can be for young people. Another quote which powerfully depicts this is found in the following interview:

IRO 6:   I'm trying to convey to them the meeting is about them and it's for them and that if people try to use the meeting as a way to criticise them or shame them then I should explain that's not the case and that shouldn't happen, especially in my reviews or the reviews I chair.

Clive: Does that happen sometimes?

IRO 6:   Yeah, sometimes you can tell. I mean, especially schools – and some carers as well – tend to bring up issues about problems and how and what he or she has done and that's not – that shouldn't be – the main centre of the meeting.

I think foster carers hold the review like a hammer over a child. It's like 'you wait 'til your father gets home'. 'You wait 'til the review. We're going to talk about this.' And so one thing that would hinder the child in the review would be allowing that kind of attitude to dominate. So you do sometimes find in a review yourself having to say to a foster carer, 'We're not going to talk about that. It's not about that. This isn't what the review's about'. It's about the IRO – that sometimes has to then be very directive, 'cos some people will insist that they talk about how shitty this kid is. …. So that can be a real hindrance, especially when they're with the foster carer all the time, and the foster carer's feeding them with ideas about reviews that are not true!

There's a sense in which children can feel quite compromised in a public space. … You kind of feel that there's a space where secrets might come out or they might betray people. They might betray their foster carers; they might betray their parents; they might betray themselves. … So that's why none of these events in a child's life are isolated.

If the child or young person has a negative experience at a review then it is understandable that they may then become reticent about attending. Many of the children and young people who come into the care system will not only have had poor experiences of parenting but also have had poor experiences of the professionals and systems that are meant to be there to protect them, and will naturally be cautious about who they can trust.

Linked to this possible reticence about participating in reviews is whether children are able to feel that they are being heard when they do participate or if they instead come away feeling that their involvement has only been tokenistic. A number of SWs acknowledged that the current system can be quite tokenistic in terms of participation by children in their review meetings. The following quote by SW 6 expresses their view of what they think participation means. In reality though, they are merely detailing the LA's responsibility under the Children Act 1989 to work in the best interests of the child. To this SW, child participation seems to mean ensuring the child understands (as far as is possible, depending on their age) the decisions made by the LA. If we relate this back to Hart's ladder of participation, it would be considered as 'tokenistic' at best; indeed, this is something the SW himself specifically acknowledges later in the interview.

SW 6:   So participation for children would mean that the child's had a level of say in what happens for them and what the Local Authority undertakes to do in the best interest of the child, and that the child should understand as well as possible for their age why decisions are made, who people are, why the meetings are there. It's very difficult because you can have participation and talk about that all you like but actually the child still remains I think …

Clive: What does that mean to you?

SW 6: Well I think that just kind of shows that a lot of what we do can be quite tokenistic. … You know, it's one thing going and getting the child's view before the review, which is what I've done, but on reflection that's still quite tokenistic. That's a visit to a child with a pre-set of questions for a meeting that isn't going to change it in structure and the actual issues can be pretty abstract and complex and they are very, very difficult to explain to a child.

The SW here is articulating the paternalistic approach espoused by many of the other SW participants, which means that they feel that the concepts considered in review meetings are too complex for children to understand and that, even if they were to see the child prior to the review, it will not impact on the way in which the meeting plays out.

Later in this interview, SW 6 reiterated how tokenistic the process was, including how the voice of the advocate carried less weight than that of the other professionals involved, and as a result, the child's voice was deemed to be less important. This is a clear example of the advocate being treated in a similarly paternalistic way as the child in the meeting. The SW then seemed to acknowledge that even the young person struggled to understand why the advocate's view was not taken as seriously as the other professionals present in the meeting:

SW 6: … the young person] was very resistant … and it made it very very difficult for her to understand why we did those things … her involvement was tokenistic because she had an advocate who would share her views but she couldn't understand why the advocate didn't carry the weight of opinion that I did or the other professionals in the room.

Clive: Were you able to be transparent with her?

SW 6:   Within the boundaries of what relationship we had, which wasn't great to be honest. Unfortunately, her mother made some terrible decisions and this particular child was probably child five out of a sequence of children that has been abused by the Local Authority, so all she ever really saw was that I thought her mum was crap.

Clive: And what would you say is the main aim of a Child in Care Review?

SW 6:   It's for the child to be listened to, for the child's voice to be heard and to ensure that we're all working together to ensure the best outcome for that child.

This response demonstrates a clear contradiction between what the SW is saying is the purpose of the meeting and what he himself acknowledges actually happens prior to and during the meeting. Arguably, this is a further example of espoused theory and theory in use (Argyris and Schön, 1974).

Structure and focus of the review not being child-centred

To effect meaningful participation the child and young person will need to be engaged during the meeting and feel that it is personal to them. In many respects the 'tick box' culture is the antithesis of this goal. SWs and IROs confirmed that reviews are used as a managerial tool and emphasized the 'tick box' organisational culture that appears to be prevalent in this LA. A central part of the IRO role is one of quality assurance: ensuring that the care plan is meeting the needs of the young person (Jelicic et al, 2014). The manner in which the IRO function is performed has the potential to either empower or disengage the child or young person:

Clive: Anything else in terms of what in your view is the main aim of the Child in Care Review?

SW 6:   To make sure that we're doing our jobs [laughs]. I think just to keep an eye on the placement as well, just to make sure that there aren't any concerns or just to make sure that all targets are being met. You know, if the social worker said they're going to do something then you know, we're doing what we said we're going to do to support that child in that placement.

This quote about the review's role being to ensure that people do their jobs properly reveals a compliance element to the review process. Essentially, it is a process to check that SWs and other professionals are doing what they should be doing – part of an audit culture and a sign of the impact of the modernisation agenda and managerialism (Featherstone et al, 2014; Diaz and Drewery, 2016). Managerialism and the modernisation agenda has led to the development of a compliance culture, belied by an obsession with completing forms on the IT system and ultimately a lack of focus on working meaningfully with children and families to help improve their lives (Munro, 2012). As Munro (2016) outlined, social work should be about helping families make positive changes to their lives rather than 'writing pretty assessments and essays'. This audit and compliance culture has been outlined by various authors (Munro, 2012; Featherstone et al, 2014; Diaz and Drewery, 2016; Forrester, 2016) as a common issue in the modern child protection system. My research suggests that review meetings are a microcosm of this checking and audit culture. For example, SW 6 stated that one of the main aims of the review is to ensure that 'all targets are being met' – a clear example of the impact of managerialism.

Through the interviews, a further barrier to children participating in their reviews emerged: the practice of holding large meetings. This issue, which was also mentioned by the IROs interviewed as part of this study, was likewise one which was previously identified in the interviews we carried out with young people in both LAs. A good example of the issues presented by large meetings was articulated by IRO 2:

Clive: What about barriers to participation? What do you think are the barriers?

IRO 2:   Large meetings. Over-formal meetings. Say, for example, if we have a meeting where there's a lot of people, a lot of professionals, and you're just reporting on what they've done and talking about what they've done or what's happened or giving their views then that's going to be very, very difficult for the child to listen to.

The practice of holding large meetings with numerous professionals in attendance was an issue that was raised by all the IROs as presenting a potential barrier to young people engaging meaningfully in their reviews. This aligns with concerns raised by young people interviewed for this research in both LAs, which concluded that young people do not like large reviews and particularly did not like schoolteachers or foster carers' SWs attending the review. It is clear that we need to look at ways of reducing the number of professionals who attend reviews.

In this study, some of the IROs said that they would ask professionals to only stay for as long as they needed to in order to say what they had to say (rather than staying for the whole meeting), while other IROs were less assertive about managing the meeting's scope. This links to the issue of who decides who is invited to attend review meetings and where and when they are held. All the IROs said that for the first review in particular, they had very little input into planning the practicalities of the meeting and the young person did not have a say in this crucial question either; instead, it all seemed to be agreed between the IRO team administrators and the SWs. All subsequent reviews would then seemingly go ahead with the same list of invitees, and again young people had very little influence over this.

The impact of young people being excluded from the process of deciding who is going to be invited to their review meeting was highlighted by IRO 6:

'I had situations when the young person became quite upset because she didn't know many people were coming to the meeting and she was wondering why they were there. So, that was an example – that young person wasn't prepared.'

Furthermore, the majority of SWs did not think that young people enjoyed or even benefited from their reviews:

SW 8:   I don't know if it's the environment or everybody sat round the table, it's quite informal, and the IRO is asking everybody specific questions – I think sometimes young people can think 'Oh my God, not me next, not me next. I don't want to talk' [laughs]. And then they feel like they just have to sometimes go along with what everybody is saying, I've noticed sometimes. And they'll speak to me after and be like 'Oh, I didn't really agree with that.'

Clive: Oh really?

SW 8:   And I say 'Well, why didn't you say at the meeting?' 'Oh no, I didn't want to cause a fuss.' So I've had that a few times. I don't know if it's because of lack of confidence or sometimes young people may feel that everybody else around them is doing their jobs and they're just fitting in. I'm not sure.

Here, the SW recognised that the meeting can be stressful – that sometimes young people do not say something because they do not want to 'cause a fuss'.

I have highlighted the barriers that exist to young people participating in their review meetings. The interviews with IROs and SWs drove home how difficult it can be to ensure that the child or young person remains the focus of the review when there are so many other competing pressures and demands at play. I will now turn to the factors which my research suggested can assist children and young people to participate in reviews.

Factors which assist participation in review meetings

So far in this chapter we have considered a number of barriers to meaningful participation. I will now outline some of the factors that the SWs and IROs identified as helping young people to participate in their reviews.

Quality of the relationship between the child and professionals

As documented in Chapter 4, all the young participants experienced a high turnover of SWs. It is worth noting that in the experience of the young interviewees in this study, if the SW showed the right attributes towards them – of taking time to get to know them, listening to them, doing what they said they were going to do and building a relationship with them – they were able to establish a trusting, effective relationship with their SW.

All the IROs acknowledged that their relationship with the young person was very important and that it was key to the young person meaningfully engaging in their review process. However, their large caseloads meant that the IROs did not get to visit children either prior to or between reviews as suggested by the *IRO Handbook* (DfES, 2010), and they all acknowledged that this had an impact on their ability to build and maintain meaningful relationships with young people.

Studies surrounding children's participation suggest that 'developing an effective procedure for eliciting children's perspectives and establishing a trusting relationship takes time' (Anderson et al, 2003, p 246). It is hard to see how such a trusting relationship can be established if IROs only see children and young people twice a year and have no contact in between reviews. All the IROs said that they would like to see young people more but that their caseloads prevented this. This aligns with the findings reported in Chapter 4, that children and young people saw the role of the IRO as chairing the meeting but they had no contact with them between reviews.

Each IRO reported a caseload in the region of 85 children, which is considerably higher than the number recommended in the *IRO Handbook* (50–70 cases). A large caseload impacts on the ability of the IRO to make visits between reviews and also to build and maintain a positive working relationship with the young person. Some of the IROs reported that they did not need long to build up a rapport with a young person and that they were able to do so in just a few minutes before a meeting. This seems unlikely and indeed is contradicted by research by Ruch et al (2012) which found that building up a trusting relationship with a young person takes a great deal of time.

SWs also raised concerns about the ability of IROs to build up relationships with young people, given that they only meet them twice a year:

> 'I wonder what he would have actually spoken truthfully to his IRO about because he took a long time to build a relationship with and a lot of intense direct work.' (SW 1)

All the SWs and IROs agreed that participation in the review process was very important for young people and that a trusting relationship with the SW and IRO was at the core of that. For example, when asked how important meaningful participation was, SW 1 stated:

> 'It's that child and it's that child's life, so they need to know what's going on and have a say, because it's them that's got to live with it every day. It shouldn't just be a tick box exercise ... it's normally done with an IRO, isn't it? So, in the hope that they have the same IRO every year that they can build a relationship with and speak honestly with, because they may have had several changes of social workers. But it's ... whether that relationship is built with them or it's just another meeting that child's got to sit in and whether they feel they can speak honestly about it. ... It can only be meaningful if that relationship [with the IRO] is actually there.'

All the SWs and IROs agreed that this concept of a positive relationship (between the IRO, SW and child/young person) was at the heart of meaningful participation. The quote also highlights the issue of the high turnover of SWs and the importance for a young person's engagement levels of having a consistent IRO. It is striking how normalised it is that young people experience a high turnover of SWs.

SW 2 also felt that meaningful participation was dependent on the young person having a meaningful relationship with the SW. When I asked SW 2 what she felt helped young people engage in their review process, she said:

> 'Making sure that the social worker's got a relationship with the child in the first place so that then the social worker is able to communicate with the child and the child is able to be open about their wishes and feelings, and be able to tell the social worker, by whatever means – it might be talking, it might be drawing or whatever – what they think about their home situation or their current living situation, and about things that are really important to them that are either really working for them or really not working for them.'

This illustrates the importance of SWs using different tools to engage children and young people and the importance of them taking time to build up that positive working relationship.

Aside from the importance of the relationship with the SW and IRO, some professionals also identified the advocate as playing a key role in assisting young people to engage meaningfully in their review meetings:

> 'I find that advocacy services have really been beneficial. I think where young people feel that they have a good relationship with an IRO as well, because obviously that's a separate part in IROs' gaining their views I think. Young people are more likely to participate if the IROs have built up a good relationship with them through the Child in Care process. I think obviously if it feels meaningful to them then if you're reviewing a Child in Care case where nothing really is changing and that child's views aren't being taken into consideration then that's going to hinder participation.' (SW 3)

This account underlines the importance of the young person enjoying positive relationships with all the professionals involved. However, we have to question how realistic it is for a young person in care to have a positive working relationship with their SW (who may have changed several times in recent years), the IRO (who often only sees them twice a year), and their advocate (who may only be offered for the first review). It is also important to consider whether the review process has developed into something which is too dependent on too many positive things occurring to make it a meaningful experience for children and young people.

When I asked the IROs to outline the factors they felt helped and hindered children and young people in engaging in the review process, they responded unanimously in saying that the quality of the relationship the child/young person has with the SW and IRO impacts upon their engagement in the review process. This is in line with previous research (Jelicic et al, 2014).

The child/young person chairing their own review meeting

As discussed in the previous chapter, the children who were most positive about their experience of review meetings were those who had chaired them. I was therefore interested in obtaining the perspectives of SWs and IROs regarding this practice.

Most IROs and SWs were positive about young people chairing their own reviews, although some expressed reservations. For example, SW 5 stated:

> 'It can go either way, can't it? It can become extremely productive, with a really engaged young person. I can think of one or two over the years that would, I think, be really switched on and really actually would have made a lot of professionals maybe buck their ideas up and maybe become a bit more child-focused. I can obviously think of one or two where they might feel it is an opportunity to rub a few people's noses in it and maybe have a bit of fun at everyone else's expense. I suppose unless you give people the chance, you never know that maybe being given that kind of responsibility could bring out the best in them. There are some young people who are or often feel quite disenfranchised.' (SW 5)

This quote implies some fear or reluctance on behalf of this SW to allow the young person to chair their own review, as there is some suggestion that they may 'abuse' the power they are given by 'rubbing people's noses in it'. This view was given (albeit less overtly) by other SWs and IROs. If the attitude expressed in the quote is shared by professionals as a whole, the result may be that children are simply not offered the choice to chair their own reviews. This ties in with George's comments in the previous chapter about having been interested in potentially chairing his own reviews but only just found out that this was an option. Since George is nearly 18 and only has one review remaining, it is likely too late for him.

However, most of the SWs were positive about young people chairing their own reviews and saw it as an effective way of facilitating meaningful participation by young people in the review process:

> 'I did a Child in Care review about six months ago where it was chaired by the young person … and he decided how he wanted to do it, and we started off by playing hangman to work out what his favourite things were … so it was completely different to how a normal Child in Care review would be. My experience would be that when things are calm and settled and straightforward then participation is thought of more. When things are falling apart or in crisis or we feel like adults need to step in and make those decisions, I would think that participation is much less then – whether that's in court proceedings or placement breakdowns, all those kind of things.' (SW 4)

Although the SW here acknowledges that participation is important, it is only realistic (both in terms of meaningful participation and in terms of the young person chairing their own review) if the placement is settled and things are going well. Therefore SW 4 clearly felt that participation was important, but when things were in crisis the adults had to take over and make the decisions for the young person to 'protect them'. It can therefore be seen that participation is not an issue when things are in harmony, but as soon as things are in crisis – which is arguably when we should be considering the young person's views the most – participation becomes a secondary concern. This echoes a finding in Thomas and O'Kane's (1999) study of almost twenty years ago, and is further evidence of a lack of progress.

There have been a number of studies into SWs' views of children's participation which have considered this particular point regarding the challenge professionals face in terms of trying to ensure young people have a voice and a role in decision making while at the same time they are kept safe. Shemmings (2000) found that SWs had a desire to 'protect children', including from 'adult decisions and discussions', and viewed this as more important than upholding children's rights to participate in decisions made about their lives, while Vis et al (2010) found that professionals often acted consciously to prevent participation by children within the child protection system. As Bessell and Gal (2009, p 287) put it: 'adults within or associated with the system tend to act as gatekeepers, determining when, if and how children's views might be treated seriously'.

While research acknowledges that children are a genuine 'resource' with something meaningful to offer society as they are 'experts' on childhood and their own lives (Hale, 2006), as this study suggests, practitioners are not always able to work in a child-focused manner which gives children the opportunity to show that they are the 'experts'.

Summary

There are several reasons why young people do not engage meaningfully in their reviews, including feeling overwhelmed by the number of professionals in attendance at the meeting, the rigid professional-based agenda and also the young people's reticence to raise their concerns due to 'not want[ing] to cause a fuss'. This aligns with the conclusions of research by Archard and Skivenes (2009, p 393), that 'children may simply lack the confidence to speak their mind even in the most favourable circumstances to the most sympathetic adults'.

This chapter has highlighted the multiple barriers which prevent children from participating meaningfully in their reviews, including the organisational culture of social work which promotes adherence to arbitrary timescales over and above supporting children–centred practice (Munro, 2012); high caseloads for SWs and IROs; limited contact between IROs and young people; the potential for reviews to become a 'blame and shame' process for young people; the high turnover of SWs; and an inexperienced workforce which appears to lack the benefit of training on participation and exhibits a lack of clarity about what 'participation' actually means, let alone how to ensure that it occurs in practice.

In terms of factors that assist children in participating in their reviews, the practice of children chairing their own reviews does offer some encouragement. This will be discussed further in the final chapter.

Notes

1   There are government requirements as to how often CiC are visited, hence the term 'statutory visit'. Individual LAs also have their own guidelines that they expect SWs to adhere to.

2   Twin-tracking, which is also known as Parallel Planning, is a term used when a contingency plan for a CiC is being explored at the same time as the primary plan for the child. As part of Permanence Planning for a CiC, Parallel Plans must be drawn up to ensure that alternative plans have been explored and are available without delay if the preferred permanent outcome proves unachievable.

6

Senior managers' perspectives

Introduction

This chapter explores the views and perceptions of the seven SMs interviewed as part of this study, all of whom came from Local Authority Two. Three of the SMs were at director level in the LA and four were Heads of Service. I was interested to ascertain the extent of their awareness and understanding of frontline practice and the challenges that SWs and IROs faced, and to discover whether they shared the same broad understanding as the other participants in relation to children's participation in their review meetings.

In the previous two chapters, I outlined some of the challenges and barriers that SWs and IROs reported in terms of children and young people participating meaningfully in review meetings. Issues were raised in relation to social work's bureaucratic processes (Munro, 2012), its relationship with information technology and the organisational culture which exists in this particular LA (which is potentially representative of the child protection system nationally). Through interviews, I sought to discover whether the SMs had a clear vision in terms of children's participation in their reviews, and in decision making and social work practice more widely. SWs, and to a lesser extent IROs, appeared not to have a clear understanding of what participation means and it was noted that very few of them had attended participation training.

An analysis of the data from the interviews with the SMs was conducted, from which a number of key themes and sub-themes emerged:

1. In relation to organisational culture and the apparent disconnect between the perspectives of SMs and other participants:
    a) understanding of the impact of high caseloads and the importance of relationships between SWs, IROs and children and young people;
    b) knowledge and understanding of the review process;
    c) understanding of participation.

2. The concept of good social work practice and the evidence base for this.

The views expressed by the SMs will be reviewed in the wider context of those of the children and young people, SWs and IROs in this study. While some convergence in views is observable, there are also some striking disparities. What follows is an exploration of each of the themes and sub-themes.

The gulf in views of SMs, frontline staff and children and young people

One theme that arose strongly when comparing the interviews of the different participants in this study was the clear disconnect which was seen to exist between what the SMs saw as the challenges within the service and the perspectives of frontline staff and children and young people. SMs' views also differed sharply from those held by the other participants in relation to the service that is offered to children, young people and their families and the impact this has on children's participation.

Barriers to building positive relationships

The young people in this study all highlighted the difficulty of building trusting relationships with their SWs, primarily because of the high turnover of staff. Many of the young participants commented on how this had impacted on their ability to participate in reviews; in the extreme, one young person said that she had refused to attend her reviews as she had such a poor relationship with her SW. They also discussed the benefits of their relationships with SWs and IROs when these were more positive and felt more genuine, rather than formulaic or guided principally by bureaucratic requirements. The young participants also highlighted feeling that some SWs lacked competence and respect for them, which was exemplified through behaviour such as by not completing tasks in a timely manner. This finding echoes research by Selwyn and Riley (2015, p 1), who found that 'maintaining and developing positive relationships are at the heart of children and young people's concerns'. Their research also maintained that:

> Rather than rushing, the young people wanted their social workers to take time to get to know them. Without this,

the young people did not feel comfortable trusting their social workers with their personal and intimate thoughts and feelings. (Selwyn and Riley, 2015, p 6)

Similarly, Godar (2015, p 13) describes the quality of relationship between children and professionals as 'crucial'. In light of this, it was surprising to note that SMs in this study rarely touched upon the importance of the SW's and IRO's relationships with children and young people, the impact of a transient workforce and the challenges SWs faced in finding the time to get to know children and young people. Indeed, SM 1 commented:

'I think it's just having people that can commit to [engage the child or young person]. I don't think that's a social work role, I think that social workers just wouldn't have time to do that, and I think you need a different skill set to do it. I'm not saying all social workers couldn't do it, I'm sure they could if they had time, but I don't really think that's the best use.'

This comment raises wider questions about what the role of a SW is, if not to engage a child or young person and put them at the heart of their practice. It is also contradictory to the body of research in this area. For example, Munro (2011, p 29) noted 'how highly children value face-to-face contact with their social workers', while Ofsted reported in 2011:

Children and young people need to be actively encouraged to express their views by someone they trust. Their social worker, or other lead professional, is best placed to ensure they are asked about their wishes and feelings. This means professionals need the knowledge and skills to communicate with children, and to understand the significance of what they are being told. (Ofsted, 2011c, p 39)

It is noteworthy, then, that SM 1 suggested this was not part of the SWs' remit and appeared to see their role as more of a case manager. SM 2 made a similar remark when asked how they thought participation could be improved if they had a magic wand:

'If money wasn't an issue, I would have someone in every team who wouldn't necessarily be a social worker, probably would come from a more youth worker type of background but a person whose role it really is to engage and also to get messages out to young people and to be the owner of that team, someone who is not burdened down with a caseload.

I don't believe that "give me another ten social workers and everything will be alright", I just believe that doing something a little bit different there would be good.'

This proposal for a youth worker in every team runs counter to the wider message from research that children and young people would prefer one stable adult professional in their lives, rather than a plethora of professionals (Selwyn and Riley, 2015). The young participants in this study were clear that it was helpful to have a consistent relationship with the same SW and IRO and that this played a key role in assisting them to participate meaningfully in their reviews. The implication of the comment is that potentially SWs do not possess these relationship skills, nor require them, and their time could be better spent elsewhere. This view appears to be due to a lack of understanding by the SM of the SW role and the way in which childcare social work teams are organised.

When discussing the potential impact that high caseloads and excessive paperwork could have on SWs having time to engage with children and young people, it transpired that SMs did not share this concern. This is exemplified in SM 2's response:

'Some of our social workers spend an awful lot of time sitting in the office doing paperwork, and we hear a lot about that, but we see other social workers who manage to balance that and do a lot more face-to-face work. We have done our own exercises to try and capture how much face-to-face work some of our social workers are doing and we understand there can be a quite significant difference and that doesn't necessarily correlate to having things like up-to-date plans and other bits of paperwork in place … sometimes you will see a lot of recordings. Texts and phone calls are all very important, but they are not an entire substitute for being sat in front of someone.'

The suggestion here is that some SWs would prefer to spend their time in front of a computer rather than with young people, a view which contrasts sharply with those views offered by the SWs in this study. For example, one SW stated in her interview that while she would rather spend time ensuring that a child who has come into care has settled into their placement, she was put under pressure by her manager and SM to fill out the 21 forms that need to be completed when a child comes into care. This SW's view was that these 21 forms contained much of the same data and that they could easily be condensed down to about 8 forms at most. Munro (2011, p 43) commented on the 'extent to which frontline workers prioritise the bureaucratic aspects of their work, and complying with performance indicators, so that finding time to spend with children and young people and create good communication comes low on the list and hence is frequently omitted'. Ultimately, it would seem reasonable to conclude that SMs were naïve about the realities of SWs' workloads and their capacity to undertake all the tasks required of them.

When SWs and IROs were asked what they would do if they were 'king of the world' and able to change one thing to improve children's participation in reviews, the resounding response was more time and lower caseloads. By contrast, the SMs wished for more focus to be placed on processes and paperwork being completed properly and on time. This evidenced a clear disconnect between the perceptions of SMs and the views of frontline staff and young people on the challenges that SWs face in relation to carrying out effective direct practice with children, young people and families. The young people interviewed also highlighted the impact of high caseloads on the service that they received. However, SMs were either not aware of this as an issue or demonstrated 'wilful blindness' towards it (Heffernan, 2014). Heffernan, who has written powerfully about the issue of wilful blindness across different sectors, argues that this may arise when SMs 'choose, sometimes consciously but mostly not, to remain unseeing in situations where we could know, and should know, but don't know because it makes us feel better not to know' (Heffernan, 2014, p 24). It is noteworthy that he suggests SMs in up to 70 per cent of all organisations are wilfully blind. Therefore, there is no moral judgement on this, and the SMs in this LA would therefore be normative in this regard.

The majority of the SMs suggested that since they observed some SWs carrying out high-quality direct work with families and completing paperwork in a timely manner, the same should be possible for all SWs. Objectively, this a simplistic view which fails to appreciate the complexity of the current challenges faced by SWs and the fact that, while some SWs may be able to carry out high-quality direct work as well as fulfilling the bureaucratic purposes of the role, they are the exception rather than the rule (Diaz and Drewery, 2016).

Frequent changes of SWs or infrequent visits by SWs to children understandably 'reduce opportunities to hear children's views and understand their experience' (Cossar et al, 2011). In their review of the IRO role in 2013, Ofsted concluded that high caseloads were a significant barrier to IROs carrying out their roles effectively (Ofsted, 2013a). SM 3 was a notable exception in her recognition of the time pressures SWs and IROs are under and the subsequent impact on children's and young people's participation:

Clive:	Do you think social workers have the time and resources to prepare young people properly for Child in Care Reviews?
SM 3:	No, I don't.
Clive:	Any reason why that is?
SM 3:	I think it's because they've just got too much work to do. I'm sure most social workers would want to give more time but I think there's lots of competing demands. … I think for real participation it is a very labour intensive, time intensive exercise and you really have to give it space. … I don't think caseload ties [and] workload management really allows and builds in enough time for that to take place properly.

While it is positive that this SM identified the issue, it was notable that, despite their position of authority and responsibility, there was no discussion as to how it was being addressed. Indeed, it was almost as if it was just accepted as normal in this LA that social work caseloads were too high for them to do their job properly but there was nothing anyone including SMs could do about this.

Some of the SMs appeared to deflect the responsibility for meaningful participation and child–centred practice onto young people themselves or individual professionals. For example, SM 1 raised the issue of children's and young people's anger towards the 'system' as a potential barrier to their participation in reviews:

'I think a lot of the barriers will be young people's perceptions of the system already and what their experiences have been, and some of that may just be anger because they haven't come to terms with it. It may not be that the system has treated them badly but, actually, the system has still interfered in their life and they may have parents in the background that are very angry at the system.

Unfortunately, the system sometimes doesn't keep its word, it says things and then it doesn't follow through. You know we keep saying to social workers how important it is when they are going to be late, that they do something about that and they make efforts to let people know, just like they would expect to be told. But I think there is a whole combination of things like that which could so easily undermine the work of saying that we care and we want to listen and all those messages.'

In a similar vein, SM 7 commented:

'If everybody was great and good at what they do then things tend to function but the barriers will often be around incompetence. Communication − social workers who don't respond to you − it boils down to social work competence practice.'

These comments tied in with a general theme which emerged in six of the seven SMs − that the faults lie with individual SWs and their poor practice. An Ofsted inspection and social work health check report carried out in this LA shortly after I conducted this research highlighted that there were issues in terms of this LA's organisational culture, and both reports stated that the LA had a 'blame culture' (Ofsted report, 2017). It could be argued that my research also points towards a blame culture within this organisation, with SMs blaming individuals for poor practice which let children down, rather than reflecting on wider organisational or systemic issues. The SMs did not reflect on their own role in 'the system' or, indeed, if an individual was undertaking demonstrably poor practice how they were challenging this. As Schooling (2016, p 15) noted: 'Where management oversight is strong there is a culture of continual challenge to improve practice at all levels. Importantly, where positive and constructive challenge is encouraged, it also helps to remove a culture of blame.' Featherstone et al (2014) identified four elements to poor organisational cultures − shaming; risk-averse audit as tyranny; distancing mechanism through technology and system design; and failing to take care of SWs − and the interviews with the SMs in this study reflected all these themes. The following comment from Forrester is of relevance to the organisational structure that appeared to be present in this LA:

> There is lots of attention paid to the management of the service with very little sense of a shared understanding of what the service is actually for. Without this the attempts to manage the system become weirdly empty. Much time and effort is devoted to activities that do not seem to have a clear purpose or likely impact. (Forrester, 2016, p 11)

I would argue that the blame culture which appears to exist in the LA research site has a direct impact on practitioners' well-being and their ability to carry out their work effectively with children, young people and their families. This is clearly a significant issue; as Morrison (2005, p 21) observed, child protection practice is 'so highly charged and emotional it is essential that middle and senior managers create a safe context for talking about doubts, uncertainty and the emotional impact of the work'.

There have been a number of studies that have raised the spectre of blame culture in children's services (Shoesmith, 2016; Leigh, 2017;). As such, this LA may not be unusual in this regard. Bennis (2009, p 38) states:

> It is essential culture of blame be avoided; instead middle and senior managers must ask staff 'how did we contribute to this mess?' This encourages a shared responsibility and shared learning.

The data suggest that SMs were not able or willing to ask themselves 'how did I contribute to this mess?' or take ownership for their cultivation of a blame culture, the effects of which cannot be minimised. The prevalence of such a culture has a severely negative impact on practice; indeed, 'the fear of being criticised or blamed for problems encourages practitioners to adopt coping mechanisms such as denial, blame and projection' (Menzies-Lyth, 1988, p 87). There was some evidence of these aspects within the SWs' and IROs' interviews, with IROs stating that they had to challenge SWs' poor practice (see Chapter 5).

SMs' knowledge and oversight of the review process

Of the seven SMs who were interviewed, only one had been to a CiC review in the last year, five had not been to one in over 20 years and one SM had never been to a review. The interview process was positive in the respect that it appeared to prompt some of the SMs to say that they now planned to go and observe a review. The responses given by SM 3 were typical:

Clive: Who do you think decides who attends the review?

SM 3:   I think that would be in discussion between the social worker and the IRO. I would like to think it also included the views of the young person but I don't know how often that happens.

Clive: And what about where the review takes place? Who do you think decides that?

SM 3:   Probably IRO and social worker but also maybe carer as well. I'd like to think it was the views of the young person but I don't know how often that happens.

There seemed to be a lack of curiosity from all the SMs in relation to what was happening in frontline practice, as illustrated in this exchange with SM 4:

Clive: Have you heard of any examples or been to places where children have chaired their own reviews?

SM 4:   I've heard that we are doing that in some areas, yeah.

Clive: But you've not actually been to one?

SM 4:   I haven't been to one, no.

When considering whether children and young people are always present at the review, SM 4 went on to comment:

> 'I don't know how many young people have to finish school early to have their reviews, I haven't got an answer to that, or whether they're always outside of school. It must be a big challenge to make sure that that is managed.'

This comment is particularly noteworthy because, in a service that is based around the needs of children, one would think it would be possible to ensure that the review occurred at a time outside of school hours. The lack of awareness is also surprising given the strong emphasis nationally on educational outcomes for children in care. The issue of reviews being in school time – with young people complaining about being called out of class and the lack of privacy – has also been documented in numerous studies (Selwyn and Riley, 2015; Mannay et al, 2017). SMs not appearing to be aware of this type of detail presents a clear challenge for improving practice within the LA. The distance from services by SMs witnessed within the study LA compares unfavourably with the position noted in Kensington and Chelsea Children's Services by Ofsted, where it was found that 'Practice leaders maintain a strong understanding of what is happening on the frontline' and 'Practice weeks have been introduced where leaders spend a week discussing cases with social workers and observing practice and, as a result, leaders know what is being done well and what could improve' (Ofsted, 2016, p 36).

In a similar vein, one SM outlined the lack of consensus and understanding SMs had about even the fundamental purpose of the review. When SM 5 was asked about the agenda for the review, she stated:

> 'I think the agenda is set by the IROs and there's a fairly standard agenda here which I now understand doesn't include reviewing the care plan. The reason given for that is that … within the children's services bit [we] aren't following the process of ensuring that the care plan is bang up to date at the point at which the review meeting is held. But I am slightly bemused by this. It's news. I only had this conversation this morning. Because I'd understood from an off-the-cuff comment that one of the service leaders made which was something along the lines of, "We've got all the emphasis on having a good care plan but the review doesn't actually review the care plan." I thought that was the purpose of the review, is the plan the right one? Are we on the right track? And apparently that's not how the agenda's set here. I had a meeting with the IRO senior manager this morning and I asked him that. He said, "No we don't. We haven't for years." So, I said, "Why is that?" and he said, "Because of all the issues that we've got about the care plan being up to date and the right care plan. So, we can't spend the meeting reviewing something that's either out of date or not relevant." When I would have thought that that's exactly what the meeting should do so that if the care plan's not right at the beginning of the review it certainly should be right at the end. But I don't want to take any more battles on really with the IROs at the moment, I'm trying to build bridges.'

According to the *IRO Handbook* (DfES, 2010), a central aim of the CiC review is to review the care plan, which – as this SM outlines – is not happening in this LA. Furthermore, despite holding the ultimate responsibility, SMs appeared to have no plans to resolve this issue. The final remark about not wanting to take on 'any more battles' with IROs evidences a fundamental lack of understanding of the current situation in this LA: it is the SWs that this SM leads that are supposed to be drafting and updating the care plans, not the IROs.

Leigh (2017) notes that where a blame culture exists, rather than pulling together to overcome perceived adversity the opposite can be seen to occur. Leigh gave the following example of what happened when staff were informed that Ofsted was coming to complete an inspection:

> The whole office has gone into meltdown. Team managers are stressed and have been seen crying. Regular trips are made to Helen's office as Helen seems to be the only one who is able to console them. I asked Helen why this is and she said it's because they don't see her as 'a threat' as she is the manager of a family support team and not a child protection team. (Leigh, 2017, p 39)

In the research site LA, there appeared to be some evidence of demarcated lines where, rather than working in collaboration, different parts of the service blamed each other for perceived failures. Likewise, IROs showed a predisposition for blaming individual SWs for their perceived incompetence.

In Chapter 5, SWs and IROs highlighted issues with form-filling and the overly bureaucratic nature of child protection practice in this LA. Previous research by Pert et al (2014) and Thomas and O'Kane (1999) has demonstrated that young people do not like filling out consultation forms since they do not see it as a meaningful way of assisting them to participate in their reviews. Some of the SMs interviewed for this study referred to the importance of written consultation forms, as evidenced in this exchange with SM 5:

Clive: Whose responsibility is it, do you think, to prepare children and young people for looked after children reviews?

SM 5: I think in the big picture it's primarily the social worker's responsibility to help young people understand what the purpose of a review is and to prepare them for what it's gonna be like – if it's in the early days – and to help prepare them to express their view and how they want to do that. To get the 'my views' written down and all of that. I think that's all within the social worker's gift.

Research has shown that children and young people do not like such forms, so the emphasis placed on this tenet by SMs is unfortunate. It was positive however that other SMs were aware that putting things down in writing was not always the best tool to use with children or young people.

SM 6 was critical of the focus on the written form and mentioned the use of new technologies as a possible solution:

'I also think another barrier is the focus still on the written form. ... I think we should use far more technology like MOMO, the advocacy app ... Skyping [and] texting. You know, the ways young people are comfortable with communicating.'

This is an interesting point, as from the point of view of a SM, the written form has the potential to provide greater accountability and is important in terms of keeping the inspectorate happy. However, this format does not necessarily respond to the needs of children and young people. This pressure on using the written form can be linked back to the comments by the young people explored in Chapter 4 about SWs asking them the same questions repeatedly, a practice which seems to show that the emphasis is on SWs obtaining the information required for their case notes, to the detriment of showing a genuine interest in the child or young person.

All seven of the SMs were aware that children and young people sometimes chaired their own reviews and appeared to view this practice as being positive. SM 2's response was typical:

'We could help them understand that the reviews are a really great place for their voice to be heard as well, around their progression, around their plan and their opportunity to take control and chair their own reviews at times, which we have seen happen in some of the older ones. ... We obviously need to try and support that as a service area to make sure we are helping young people to feel confident enough to chair their own reviews and see what we can do to support that side of it.'

SM 1 similarly commented:

> 'What I would hope it does is build the young person's confidence in the review and [see] that the review is actually about them and that their voice is central and important within this review. For that reason, I would like to see young people chair it because the worry is that a young person will go to a review and there is a group of adults around and they sit there very passively, very quietly, and we won't necessarily hear what they want to say to us. Then it's a missed opportunity, so I think that more than anything is the reason and also that there are lots more skills and confidences that they will build by taking a bit of control and chairing their review or were part of the review.'

It was interesting that for some of the SMs, who had lengthy careers in the sector, the idea of young people chairing their own reviews was not a novel one. Furthermore, it was noteworthy that for many of these SMs it appeared that not much had changed or improved in relation to children participating in reviews:

Clive:	How effectively do you think we engage young people in their reviews?
SM 5:	Most of my career it was terribly variable. I'd say I went through periods when kids hardly ever went to their reviews 'cos again I think the culture of the organisation was if they don't wanna sit in there they don't have to. So, I think it's still very variable and I think our understanding is probably still quite variable about the extent to which children are at the heart and young people are at the heart of their meeting.

These comments suggest that there is an acceptance that things are just the way they are and there are no plans to address this issue. SM 5 mentioned the time when she worked in a residential children's home and the young people had decided to chair their own review meetings, and went on to comment:

> 'Well, that example that I gave you, that will have been about 28 years ago. Now I don't think we've made progress since then really. That was practice 28 years ago and we're

still in a situation where we've got a handful of kids chairing their own meetings.'

Dickens et al (2014) found that, despite the heightened discourse around child-centred practice, the proportion of children attending their reviews has not changed significantly in the 18 years since Thomas and O'Kane (1999) carried out their study. The acceptance of 'variable' practice as articulated in this interview was further demonstrated in all the SM interviews, where they seemed to have low expectations of social work practice in relation to engaging and carrying out effective child-centred practice. For example:

Clive: If you had a magic wand and you could do anything to improve children's participation in Child in Care reviews, what would it be?

SM 7:   I would want everyone to know what they are doing and that they do things in a timely manner – that might help improve reviews.

Understanding of participation

The previous chapter demonstrated that most SWs did not have a good understanding of what 'participation' really means. IROs demonstrated a greater knowledge but bemoaned the lack of training in this area. Given the strategic role of SMs, I was interested to interrogate their understanding of the term 'participation', since, arguably, without SMs having a good understanding of this concept, it is difficult for them to drive forward any improvement in this essential area of practice.

During my interviews with the seven SMs, it became apparent that their understanding was potentially superficial and that tokenistic participation was deemed 'good enough'. The SMs used buzzwords but there was no mention of research or what evidence suggests 'works'. The following comment from SM 3 illustrates the manner in which participation was considered:

'So, I suppose the overarching thing is that we want to know and understand what the views of children are and that can be on a personal basis, on a day-to-day social work basis. But it can also be on a service development basis. So, there's also an effort to try and get the views of young people when we're making decisions about how we deliver services. And participation for me means that we ask children what their views are, whatever the level, that we ensure that those views are included in the consultation process or whatever it is and then we tell the children what the outcome of that was after. That would be my view of what is participation.'

When considered in relation to Hart's 'ladder' of participation, the notion of children being told of the outcome of the consultation process after it has concluded clearly places their participation at a low level, which is out of step with the restorative principles and empowering goals of working with young people and their families (Stanley and Featherstone, 2015). This observation is significant: for the 12 months preceding this study, the LA in question had invested significant funds in trying to embed Restorative Practice principles and all SMs and most IROs had been on a three-day course on Restorative Practice (LA agency report, 2017).

Another example came from SM 5:

Clive: In general terms, what does participation mean to you?

SM 5:   It means that children and young people are fully engaged with – if we're talking about participation – with us. Fully engaged in our system. That they've been properly involved in understanding why we're involved, what we're doing, that they've been empowered to express a view about what they want and what their important things are, that they're empowered to express that in different forms.

Despite talk of empowerment, the language used by this SM refers to children and young person being fully engaged in 'our' system, thus reflecting the 'tokenistic participation' stage of Hart's (1992) 'ladder'. We can link this back to Munro's (2012) assertion that social work is about 'doing the right thing not doing things right'. In this LA, the interviews with the SMs indicated that their management style was based on the technical rational approach:

As many commentators have noted, safeguarding and social work practice with children and families over recent decades has been dominated by a technical, rational approach to practice … the development and introduction of procedures, checklists and processes as a way of managing the increasing volume and complexity of the work and to assist practitioners to predict and minimise risk. (Earle et al, 2017)

Troublingly, this approach is not confined to this particular LA. Indeed, as Broadhurst et al (2009, p 359) found in research conducted across five LA areas, 'workers consistently claimed that it was easy to lose sight of the primary activities of supporting families and safeguarding children, to the second-order activities of performance and audit'. This is epitomised by the competing priorities of 'putting (data) in' and 'going out' to see families (Peckover et al, 2008, p 139).

One SM demonstrated a relatively limited understanding of the meaning of participation:

Clive:	If you had a magic wand and there's something … that could improve children's participation in Child in Care reviews, what would it be?
SM 4:	I'd like to be certain that every professional going to a review understands exactly what they're there for and what their role is. Because if everyone does that then it should be a good experience.

Role clarity, though important, does not in itself impact necessarily on children's participation in review meetings or indeed on wider practice. This answer suggests potentially low expectations of social work practice; furthermore, it is noteworthy that the SM made no reference to children in the response. This SM further commented:

Clive:	Do you speak to staff about participation generally? What would your messages be in relation to that?
SM 4:	[T]he conversations we've had, or I've had, have been this kind of thinking about participation and thinking about direct work of children and the potential difference. So, understanding a child's experience, understanding their lived experience – what's it like being them – is kind of direct work and listening. Now some teams say that's child participation but I think that's slightly different. At a team day recently, young ambassadors were there talking about their experience. That's participation, isn't it? … So, I think it's complex; I don't think it's … and I think

in our … in social care maybe that gets mixed up
a bit.

The somewhat garbled nature of this response is symptomatic of the issue at play here. This SM's insight into participation is derived purely from a group session at a team day, rather than from leading something which is embedded into the everyday practice of working with individual children and young people. Furthermore, this appears to be the only direct experience related to participation that SM 4 has been involved with, further underscoring the observations in Chapter 5 about SMs' lack of knowledge of and involvement with the reality of practice on the frontline. There is not a direct strategy to enable the participation of children and young people in their reviews.

In stark contrast to the views articulated by the SWs and IROs, six of the seven SMs seemed to think that when participation (or their understanding of participation at least) did not happen properly for young people, this could not be seen to be a result of high caseloads or issues with the bureaucratic nature of the system. Instead, SMs took the line that SWs did not 'get it' in some way and that the issue was that SWs preferred to spend their time behind a computer screen, filling out forms, rather than carrying out direct work with young people.

The concept of 'good social work practice' and the evidence base

Over the last 30 years, social work has embarked on a professionalisation drive (Howe, 2014). Despite this, the professionals interviewed in this study still seemed to display limited knowledge of what we mean by good social work practice and how to carry it out. As Munro (2016) outlines, the central aim of social work should be helping families change; unfortunately, in practice the focus appears to be complying with bureaucratic processes, and ultimately paying lip service to the children and families who should be at the heart of practice (Diaz and Drewery, 2016).

The previous two chapters presented data indicating that SWs and IROs were in a state of crisis, where high caseloads meant that they were too busy 'fire-fighting' to reflect meaningfully on their work with children and families. This led to a disconnect between what they said was important – children's participation – and what happened in practice. When discussing in more detail the practicalities of the meetings (such as who set the agenda, who chose who was invited, and where and when the meeting took place), it became evident that young people played little to no role in deciding these aspects and that their level of participation was ultimately only tokenistic. Further, it was demonstrated that SWs struggled to understand in depth their practice and the potential impact of this on young people and their families. The data suggest that SWs lacked the tools to know how and what could be done to implement meaningful participation.

It has been argued that although SWs are enthusiastic in relation to the notion of evidence-based practice and agree that their work would be more effective if it were informed by evidence, when questioned, the majority are not able to name an evaluative study or piece of research (see also Sheldon and Chilvers, 2002). The same can be said of SMs; when asked about what they believed 'worked' or what evidence suggests is good practice in relation to children's meaningful participation, the SMs in this study were not aware of any up-to-date research or evidence. These interviews with SMs suggested a lack of understanding of evidence-based or evidence-informed practice and the ways in which this could be embedded into the work carried out with families.

The data suggested an overemphasis by management on 'management tasks'. Munro (2011, p 44) suggests that managers need to take responsibility for improving practice, and furthermore, they 'need to create the space and priority to allow it to happen'. The following exchange with SM 3 illustrates this point:

Clive:	Overall, just thinking about it from your role, do you think IROs generally have helped improve outcomes or permanence for children and young people, not just in terms of participation but more widely?
SM 3:	That's quite a difficult question isn't it? I think, well if I'm saying to you that I think the experience of the review is better now than it was then I'm sure the IRO must have had a role in that. Whether outcomes for young people are better now than they were prior to IROs I think that's a very difficult one and I don't know if I could say whether they are or not really. I suppose evidentially with children in care prospects are no better now than they were ten, fifteen years ago overall. I don't know.
Clive:	Are they not?
SM 3:	That's what we hear.

Clive:	Have they not got any better in the last fifteen, twenty years?
SM 3:	I don't know.

This comment indicates that there is limited evaluation of the services that are being delivered in this LA. SWs are finding it increasingly difficult to comply with their administrative requirements alongside their task of understanding what a child's life is like and then delivering appropriate and effective support (Burgess et al, 2013; Holmes and McDermid, 2013). IROs face similar time pressures, but equally, their focus sometimes seems to be on criticising the SW for not completing all tasks. Meanwhile, the SMs appear to have a limited understanding of the perspectives of frontline SWs and what good social work should look like.

Summary

Through this chapter's examination of the SMs' views, it has become apparent that SMs are distanced from the review process and, crucially, have a poor understanding of the pressures faced by SWs. It is remarkable and very concerning that the young people interviewed in this LA appeared to have a better understanding of the pressures faced by SWs as a result of too high and too complex caseloads. Furthermore, SMs did not even seem to think there was an issue with SWs having high caseloads and they blamed any practice issues on individual SWs' incompetence. This disconnect between SMs and frontline SWs is very concerning, especially as the SMs did not appear to have a clear understanding of the concept of participation. There appeared to be a general air of acceptance about a 'system' that would not change.

7

When it goes wrong

Despite the introduction of guidelines and procedures aimed at encouraging and supporting children and young people to complain about services which they feel dissatisfied with, children in care still face barriers to doing so in practice. This chapter explores the complaints procedure for children in care and discusses the experience for both children and professionals, how children can express their views about their care and also how this process is managed by professionals.

The field work for the research reported in this chapter was carried out in Local Authority Two. We conducted semi-structured interviews with children in care, SWs, SMs and IROs, and five distinct themes emerged:

1. Complaints by children in care are managed at the lowest possible level.
2. SMs have an overly optimistic view about children in care being informed of complaint procedures and being encouraged to do so.
3. Children in care are worried about complaining, which is recognised by professionals.
4. Children's voices are often not heard.
5. When issues are clearly defined, IROs have some degree of success in resolving complaints from children in care.

Children in care: a demographic

Most children in care have experienced trauma or maltreatment during their lifetime (Wade et al, 2011). It is therefore imperative that – as with all children – they are provided with stable and loving homes: homes where the rules and boundaries are fair and clear. Furthermore, children in care must feel a sense of belonging, an age-appropriate sense of empowerment, control over their own destiny and the deserved feelings of love and value (Pert et al, 2014)

The mental health of looked after children is significantly poorer than that of their peers; shockingly, almost half meet the criteria for a psychiatric disorder. To put this in perspective, only one in ten of non-looked after children suffer from a diagnosed mental health disorder (Luke et al, 2014). In 2017, almost one in ten children in care surveyed by Ofsted reported that their foster carers, or professionals within children's residential homes, rarely or never comforted or assisted them when they were upset (Ofsted, 2017).

Given these statistics, it is perhaps unsurprising – though nonetheless deeply concerning – that children in care and care leavers continue to have some of the worst outcomes of all children in the UK (Berridge et al, 2015). Almost one third of children in care leave school with no qualifications (Mannay et al, 2017), and a disproportionate number of children in care and care leavers end up part of the criminal justice system (The Who Cares? Trust, 2016).

This chapter will discuss the reasons behind the dissatisfaction of children with social services and explore the impact upon children of such failures to meet their needs.

Complaining: a social construct

In general terms, the very act of complaining carries social stigma. There is a fear attached to the process of complaining: we fear being characterised as rude or impolite when we attempt to highlight our dissatisfaction (Cowan and Halliday, 2003; George et al, 2007). There is a well-established evidence base which suggests that the more disadvantaged a person is, the poorer the service is that they receive. Moreover, the process of complaining, and one's ability to do so, has a direct correlation with socio-economic status. Best and Andreasen (1977) posited that high-socio-economic status households were more likely to complain, due, in part, to either greater access to resources or a higher sense of self-worth. Hirschman (1970) demonstrated that individuals who were more capable of leaving an organisation were also more effective at voicing their complaints. In contrast, disadvantaged groups in society, particularly those unable to exit a service (such as social services), invariably feel that they should be grateful for any service they receive. Consequently, they often resign themselves to the expectation that they will not receive a fair service that meets their needs (George et al, 2007).

Research by Lipsky in the 1970s and 1980s found that 'poor people receive a qualitatively different kind of treatment from the state' and that because this is non-voluntary for many of these clients, professionals had 'nothing to lose by failing to satisfy clients' (1980, p 54). Children are even less likely to challenge the service they receive and tend to accept what adults tell them (Pert et al, 2014).

Complainants are most satisfied when the organisation responds flexibly and quickly to their complaint (Hanna, 1992). Complaints are rectified best when complaint procedures are effective, that is, when they are impartially administered or when an independent or layperson is included in the process. Service users have expressed that they wish to be believed by the organisation, in hopes that their complaint will change practice in the future (Donaldson and Cavanagh, 1992; Mulcahy and Lloyd-Bostock, 1994). In public services such as children's social care, it is particularly important that complaints procedures are effective, clear, accessible and well managed so that trust between the service and service user can be built and maintained. Since service users have little choice in the services they receive and may not be able to exit the service at all, it is key that the relationship between the two is preserved as much as possible when a grievance occurs (Goodman–Delahunty et al, 2013).

The history of complaints procedures for children

The Children Act 1989 formalised the right of children in care to complain. This was in part an attempt to reduce the abuse of children in institutional care and to counter the perception that the abuse of children in care had continued because their complaints were not being heard (Levy and Kahan, 1991). A power imbalance exists between children and the professionals who support them, a reality that is extensively supported by research, which identifies that children and young people feel they have little power and perceive SWs as holding control (Farnfield, 1998; Munro, 2001; Barnes, 2009). In practice, this results in children remaining silent despite dissatisfaction or even when incidents of abuse have occurred. It is clear therefore that children must be, or feel, empowered before they can be expected to effectively engage with a complaint procedure.

During a debate in the House of Lords in 1989, Lord Meston described complaints as being a social construct designed to enable the continuity of relationships, rather than, say, being purely a mechanism of redress. He said:

> There should be a specific complaints procedure to deal with matters, which may be relatively trivial or serious, that need to be ventilated and redressed, but which perhaps are not appropriate matters to put before the court. (Hansard HL Deb, 17 January 1989, p 175).

Thus, he argued there were three reasons for implementing complaints procedures:

1. to enable problems to be diffused easily and quickly;
2. to maintain standards of service delivery;
3. to protect children.

The Children Act 1989 enshrined the concept and legal right of children and young people to complain about the service they receive. The Act dictated that children's wishes and feelings should be ascertained and considered in the provision of services, and Section 26 of the Act specifically introduced the requirement that LAs should establish complaints procedures. Roche (1999) and Lowden (2002) argue that this specific section was rash because in 1989 adults still failed to adequately acknowledge the rights of children. Indeed, children's involvement and participation in the services and decisions that affect their lives continue to be underplayed. The concept that a complaint is a useful quality and feedback measure was also deemed to be premature, as researchers noted that this was still not welcomed by LAs (Waterhouse, 2000). The Waterhouse Report into sexual abuse in care homes (conducted in Wales between 1974 and 1990) also highlighted that children do not complain due to feelings of embarrassment or shame, or because they lack full understanding of the severity of events that occurred or fear reprisal, and, as such, may be 'justified' in their cynicism towards complaint handling (Waterhouse, 2000, pp 426–7).

Consequently, the mechanisms for children to complain were reconsidered in the Adoption and Children Act 2002, which introduced the post of the independent reviewing officer (IRO) whose role it is to ensure that looked after children's care plans meet their needs. If an IRO is unhappy about a care plan, and they have been unable to resolve this with the team manager informally or during reviews, then they can raise their concern with the CAFCASS. However, this mechanism is rarely used: as of February 2015, there had only been ten referrals by IROs to CAFCASS (Dickens et al, 2015). Ten referrals in 13 years, particularly given what we know about some of the services that children in care receive, is remarkably low.

IROs also have the option to raise concerns with the inspectorate Ofsted as well as with the Children's Commissioner. IROs are required to ensure children know about the complaint procedure in each LA (*IRO Handbook*, ch. 6, DfES, 2010) and they should support young people to make complaints when they deem it appropriate. A potential overlap exists between complaints procedures and the dispute resolution processes that are in place in LAs, which IROs can use to challenge practice. There is increased scrutiny over the efficacy and independence of the IRO service, and the fostering stocktake report commissioned by the Department of Education has even gone so far as to suggest that LAs should be able to abandon the IRO role (Narey and Owens 2018). At the time of writing, the government disagreed with this proposal and for the moment at least the IRO role appears safe.

Under the Adoption and Children Act 2002, a requirement was introduced for LAs to provide an advocate to those children making a complaint. The subsequent policy supporting this Act was the 2004 'Every Child Matters' document. This purported that 'vulnerable children and young people [should] get the help they need, when they need it, however small or large their complaint' (DfES, 2004, p 5). A key tension, however, is that advocacy services are commissioned by LAs through ongoing contracts, and hence, service providers risk losing the contract (or perceive that they will) if they vociferously challenge LAs.

A new standardised format for how LAs should deal with complaints was introduced in Representative Procedures (England) 2006. This is partitioned into three stages:

Stage 1: Informal Complaint. The complainant should receive an acknowledgment of their complaint along with details of the complaints procedure and advice on obtaining an advocate. The LA must appoint one of their officers who must try to resolve the complaint within ten working days.

Stage 2: Formal Registered Complaint. The LA must appoint an independent person to consider the representations. Investigations should be completed within 25 days.

Stage 3: Review Panel. The LA organises a review panel that consists of three independent persons. The panel compiles a written report and the LA must, within 15 days of receiving the report, determine what they propose to do and inform the complainant.

A clear contradiction is observable within this system. It is well established that many children in care feel unhappy with the service they receive, but despite the fact that making a complaint has arguably never been easier for children now that advocacy services are available and there is legislation and policy in place, the number of complaints registered by children in care remains stubbornly low. Since national statistics on complaints from looked after children are not published, the best indication of their rate of occurrence comes from Ofsted's 2012–13 statistics on fostering. From the data submitted by all 152 LAs across England, a total of 216 complaints were reportedly received from children in foster care, which equates to 0.4 per cent of the 53,369 children reported to have been placed in foster care that year. Of the 216 complaints made by children and young people, LAs reported that 87 (40 per cent) were not upheld. (UK Government, 2014).

Both children and adults face barriers to complaining to LAs. To counter this issue, the Commission for Local Administration in England, in conjunction with the Local Government Ombudsman, produced guidance on good practice for running a complaints system (Local Government Ombudsman, 2009). The first key tenet of this guidance is that councils should make complaints systems accessible for their clients. The guidance encourages councils to provide visual information for those with learning difficulties or literacy problems, making systems accessible to children and young people, and while it is not specifically mentioned, the inference is that the information should be accessible for those for whom English is not a first language. The guidance is clear that it is 'not a question of meeting minimum requirements but of taking an imaginative and informed approach' (Local Government Ombudsman, 2009, p 6).

While access to information and communication has become widely universal, there are still some residual issues around making such information accessible to clients of all ages and backgrounds (Keegan Eamon and Kopels, 2004). LAs, due to financial pressures, have tended to centralise their complaints services into one corporate complaints system. This can make it more difficult for children in care to access the complaints service, especially where the complaints form is generic and held on the Corporate Services section of the website rather than under Children's Social Care.

Even where children do complain, it is thought that many grievances expressed by children are not recorded as complaints but, rather, treated as informal service requests or feedback. This process of diverting complaints is legitimised on the basis that grievances are being resolved, but without a formal acknowledgment of grievances, or independent evaluation of them, there is no evidence of their resolution (Neil, 2015). This also makes it difficult in terms of compiling statistics on the numbers of complaints made by children in care. The Local Government Ombudsman (2009, p 4) asserted: 'There is no difference between a formal and informal complaint. Both are expressions of dissatisfaction that require a response.' This is not to suggest that every concern should be treated as a formal complaint, as, indeed, children do just want someone to listen sometimes and it is desirable for complaints to be resolved informally where possible (McLeod,

2000; Pinkney, 2013). Mediation and resolution, undertaken as close to the source of the complaint and as swiftly as possible, may well lead to a better outcome and ultimately be more satisfactory for children. However, the lack of complaints by children in care against the system means it is difficult to ascertain the level of complainants' satisfaction (Mulcahy and Tritter, 1998; Simons, 1995).

Complaints often centre on an individual feeling they have not been listened to. McLeod (2000) argues that children and SWs have different perceptions and experiences of what constitutes 'listening'. Hence, even when SWs are focused and engaged in what they designate to be 'listening', children do not believe that they are being heard; this is borne out by a growing body of research (O'Quigley, 2000; Sinclair, 2004; Duncalf, 2010). Other research has demonstrated that children and young people are concerned about the potential impact complaining might have on their relationship with their SW (Carmel, 1988). Children have a propensity to feel guilty or blame themselves for difficult situations; this is likely to be keenly felt by children in care who have experienced breakdown of their family and often blame themselves. Children feeling unable to voice their concerns can have long-term emotional effects, as they may blame themselves for not being confident enough to speak up when unhappy (Muench et al, 2017).

There is a paucity of research on complaints by children in care, which is possibly related to the limited nature of data on complaints (Neill, 2015; Muench et al, 2017). Where complaints data are available, a recurrent theme is the emphasis on meeting deadlines and targets. Monitoring is geared towards quantitatively measurable statutory objectives, including timescales for completing bureaucratic duties (Clarke et al, 2000; Ofsted, 2013a). This means that professionals may be tempted to place greater emphasis on adhering to timescales, rather than learning from complaints on a qualitative level.

Researching the perspectives of children and professionals

The purpose of this research was finding out how professionals working with children in care view and manage complaints. We were also interested in knowing what happens when children in care complain and specifically what young people and professionals think happens when complaints are made.

Ten young people, 11 SWs, 8 IROs and 7 SMs were interviewed in Local Authority Two. All participants were asked specifically about complaints made by children in care and how these were managed.

Semi-structured interviews were conducted with both young people and professionals. The young people were aged between 11 and 17.

All ten children reported that, at times, they had a SW (or, in some cases, numerous SWs) who had not treated them well. All of them stated that complaining would have made their situation worse. It is also important to stress here that most of the young people also reported working with 'good' SWs.

What we found

Data from the young participants in this study were triangulated with the views of professionals interviewed, all of whom had experience of young people making complaints. It is acknowledged at the outset that a weakness of this study was the fact that we were unable to interview young people who were specifically known to have made formal complaints, and it is suggested that future research addresses this. This was partly because so few children in care in that LA had made complaints; out of over 600 children in care at the time of the research only 3 had made complaints in the last twelve months and they were not willing to be interviewed for this research.

Complaints by children in care are minimised

Frustration was expressed by all of the young people, SWs and IROs interviewed that complaints by children were not being taken seriously enough. The following exchange with an IRO, talking about a 16-year-old whose placement was moved in an unplanned manner, illustrates this:

IRO 2:   Our EDT [emergency duty team] got involved because … the child was refusing to go in. She was sixteen years old. And eventually she went in at two o'clock in the morning. I went down to see her a few weeks later and actually put a complaint together for her because she said she wanted to complain. She felt the way she'd been treated was really, really bad. And I agreed. [We] put the complaint in. And, of course, it was dealt with at Stage One. She got an advocate. … She didn't get a satisfactory answer. She got a kind of half-hearted apology from the deputy team manager. She wanted to go to Stage Two with the advocate. They wouldn't have it.

Clive:	Who decides that?
IRO 2:	The complaints manager.
Clive:	And can they just say no?
IRO 2:	Yeah. It seems so.

What is striking about this particular example is that the young person knew the service she received was unacceptable; other children may not have come to the same realisation. Despite this, she was thwarted in her attempt to complain and have her voice heard in a manner that allowed her to feel the issue had been properly dealt with.

IRO 1 commented: 'In the end the child just gives up.' This feeling of futility likely has a marked emotional impact on children in care, who have not only been let down by their families but also then by the state. This example also raises questions about the efficacy of advocates and advocacy services, as there is no evidence to suggest that the advocate appealed – formally or otherwise – the decision not to allow the young person to progress to Stage Two with an advocate.

Some professionals felt that keeping things 'at a low level' was the most appropriate course of action, and that their professional discretion could determine whether the matter should be escalated or not:

> 'If a specific issue comes up, or usually in my chat with the young person before the meeting starts, I talk with them about if they're not happy what they can do about it. So that might be bringing the social worker in and saying "what are we going to do about this?" … If I feel it's more significant, I might think with them more about the role of an advocate and I've referred loads of people for advocates in my time.' (IRO 4)

The difficulty with professional discretion being used in this manner is that it is not empowering for children or young people, because they are still restricted in the information shared with them while decision making about the validity of their complaint remains subject to gatekeeping by a professional.

Children are fearful about making a complaint

A recurrent theme in the interviews with young people was that they worried about speaking up. Every young person referred to having 'stayed silent' at some point when in care, because saying something either felt too difficult or just futile as they would not be listened to:

Clive   Okay, so you've had one social worker the whole time.

George: Yes, that was more because I was too afraid to challenge him and change to a different one though.

Despite some of the young people holding very negative views of some of their SWs, they still did not consider complaining. For example:

Charmaine: I didn't like my first one. I hated her. She was terrible. She didn't get anything done at all. For the whole six weeks holidays in the summer I wanted to stay at my friend's house to be like a normal person. I asked her to get my friend's house police checked and everything so I could stay there and six weeks later she still hadn't done it. She would always be late.

Clive: Did you consider making a complaint about this social worker?

Charmaine: No, there would have been no point; it would have just made things worse.

Professionals working directly with children and young people expressed how difficult it was for children and young people to complain. For example, IRO 1 referred to one young person who spoke up as 'brave':

> 'One time, years and years ago, there was a boy in a foster placement and his social worker wasn't any good, and he was brave enough to say so and he made a formal complaint.'

Four of the seven SMs interviewed endorsed the notion that children were right to be worried about complaining, as their experience dictated that there were times when making a complaint impacted upon a child's relationship with their SW:

SM 1:   In a small minority of cases the social worker has taken it as an offence that there's been a complaint and has then complained to the young person which is not on.

SM 7:   He said, well my social worker told me off for complaining because he got him into trouble. So yes, I think it is a difficult one for young people to [complain].

The most troubling aspect of these exchanges is the 'blame culture' it appears to belie: while young people worry about complaining, SWs are concerned about being blamed when a child they are working with complains. The knock-on effect is that children are left not feeling confident enough to challenge decisions they are unhappy with.

Children's voices are not heard

In instances where young participants voiced opinion, they reported feeling that they were not listened to and expressed variously 'I had no choice', 'I wasn't asked my opinion', and so on. It is noteworthy that all of the SWs surveyed as part of this study reported that children's and young people's views could be disregarded and, moreover, that agency processes enabled this:

> 'I don't always think we're that good at allowing children and young people to say what they want if it's in conflict to what's written. I think we take that away from them because it's that "they're in care, we need to protect them, we need to make these decisions for them", and I think that comes down to again the view that it's statutory, it's bureaucratic, and we're there to set things and put things in motion, and we're not as flexible as we should be, and we maybe don't say to children and young people "this is a plan that we've put in place" or "we need to look at a plan for this, let's do it together".' (SW 11)

Here, SW 11 shows insight into the way the system is designed to operate: bureaucracy takes precedence, to the detriment of facilitating discussions with the child or young person to ensure that they are able to play an active role in the decisions that are made about their lives.

Another SW reported that children and young people may be unable to get their views heard:

> '[The young person's] involvement was tokenistic because she had an advocate who would share her views, but she couldn't understand why the advocate didn't carry the weight of opinion that I did or the other professionals in the room.' (SW 6)

What is particularly interesting about this comment is the assumption by the SW that their opinion and that of other professionals in the room should carry more weight than the advocate or the young person. Indeed, this assumption is so ingrained that the SW provided no explanation for why this was the case.

In terms of the young people's views of review meetings, most of them found them boring and pointless and sometimes scary. Despite this, none of them considered complaining about this as they felt it would just make things worse.

IROs' roles in resolving issues

Most of the young people stated that at times IROs were able to resolve fairly straightforward matters such as ensuring young people saw a dentist regularly but they were less effective at resolving more complex issues such as contact with siblings.

> 'Like my health checks would be sorted, … the day-to-day schooling would be sorted, but when it came to contact … the IRO would help me try and get it but it's obviously not her decision, that's up to the social worker.' (Kiera)

In contrast to SWs and SMs, overall, IROs appeared to be more responsive to children's needs and showed greater recognition of the importance of children's voices being heard. IROs reflected upon the impact of children not being listened to:

> 'It can get quite challenging sometimes. Young people storm out of meetings. … I'm sure a lot of the time there'd be themes to those scenarios which are about not feeling heard.' (IRO 5)

Several IROs were able to cite examples of when they had advocated on behalf of a child or young person. Where the issue was narrow and clearly defined, most had examples of success. This was exemplified by IRO 5's account of a young person with very few clothes who was living on a Care Order with her mother:

> 'We had a meeting downstairs with her mum and everybody, and the girl lost it … because I'd said to her, "Do you want an advocate?" "No". "Do you want me to do something about it?" "Yes". "Well, there's a limit to what I can do about it, but I'll do my best, and if I can't, then we'll talk about an advocate." … Why didn't I do that before? I was

quickly able to get the senior manager to agree money for some clothes but it's difficult. When I've got 50. I work three days a week. ... So now I'm making it my business.'

IRO 3 discussed the role that IROs can play in helping children at least feel that their voices have been heard, even if they do not get the desired outcome:

'I think [IROs are] probably quite successful ... because quite often we know about those concerns prior to the review, especially if you've spent any time with the child, so we can bring it up on their behalf. We can then talk about it openly then because we set decisions at the review.'

The disparity in attitudes between SWs and IROs regarding the importance of the child's voice calls into question the proposal by the fostering stocktake (Narey and Owens, 2018) to disband the IRO role. It can be discerned from the preceding discussion that SWs can be seen to be more attached to the bureaucracy, more fearful of a blame culture and less able to exercise professional discretion, while IROs appear more confident in their professional views, perhaps because a key part of their role is oversight of the care plan and challenging poor practice (Dickens et al, 2015).

Management of complaints by professionals working with children in care

Our study found that complaints by children in care were managed at the lowest possible level and that professional discretion was exercised to determine whether complaints should be escalated via formal procedures. Consequently, even when children were aware of their right to make a complaint, they encountered barriers to exercising this right. The young people interviewed for our study all stated that while there were things they felt dissatisfied about, they did not complain because they were concerned about making things worse. These findings are in accordance with Parry et al (2008) and Dickens et al (2014), who found that SWs and team managers often played a gatekeeping role with respect to complaints and tended to downplay complaints in order to resolve issues outside of formal procedures. Indeed, some professionals pointedly avoid the use of formal complaints mechanisms because they view them to be a 'pointless and unnecessary layer of bureaucracy' (Parry et al, 2008, p 14).

Furthermore, our study found that even when children in care did complain, their voice did not carry equal weight to that of the professionals and, consequently, they were not always listened to. As aforementioned, earlier research has highlighted how children and young people can feel powerless in their relationships with SWs (Farnfield, 1998; Munro, 2001). As Adams et al note, 'the power and status imbalance is firmly with the worker who is advantaged as a representative of the state' (2009, p 16). While this imbalance was recognised by SWs workers in the present study, it was viewed as simply being 'part of the system'. These findings are in accordance with Barnes' (2009) study, in which interviewed SWs also recognised the presence of a power imbalance between themselves and young service users, but saw this as relatively unproblematic and even natural in light of the fact that children and young people are 'immature' and 'dependent upon adults' (Barnes, 2009).

A commitment to anti-oppressive practice is central to core social work values (BASW, 2012) and this includes the empowerment of children and young people. However, SWs may encounter difficulties in achieving the right balance between working in collaboration with children and young people and exercising their powers to protect them (Cossar et al, 2016). SWs (and other professionals) should be mindful of this in their work with children and young people (Cossar et al, 2016), so that 'the imbalance be negotiated in a manner least likely to be oppressive' (Adams et al, 2009, p 22). Furthermore, as previously noted, not feeling listened to has the potential to have a negative emotional impact on children in care, since it may 'compound or reactivate [the] feelings of powerlessness' (Cossar et al, 2016, p 104) that were triggered by being removed from their family and placed in care.

Children's reluctance to complain

The findings from our study also underscore the point that children are reluctant to make complaints against social services as they perceive this to be either pointless or too difficult. These findings resonate with Pithouse and Crowley's (2007) research, which found that young people did not complain because they felt as though they were not listened to or taken seriously by professionals. Similarly, Barnes (2009) posited that children may refrain from complaining about social services as they feel 'it is not worth it'. Moreover, Neill (2015) found that children often find alternative methods of resolving their issues or grievances that may, in fact, prove quicker and more effective.

For example, a child who is unhappy in their placement may go missing, self-harm or display violence against their carer to force a placement breakdown.

Although it is positive that some of the professionals interviewed in our study recognised and understood the difficulties children face in making complaints, it is concerning that the majority of the SMs felt that children were justified in being worried about complaining due to the negative impact this could have upon the child–SW relationship. The findings of this study suggest that this may be due to the existence of a 'blame culture' in which SWs are fearful of being blamed when a child they are working with makes a complaint. The suggestion here then is that SWs – to some extent – have to keep the child on board and, as Lipsky (1980, p 54) noted, keep clients compliant. This does not engender a positive learning culture where children's and young people's needs are considered a priority.

In the broader research carried out for this book, it has been noted that SMs take little responsibility for service failings; instead, they appeared to blame individual SWs for poor practice. The Munro Review of Child Protection (2011) argued that SWs need to assert their professional standing and develop their expertise in working with families and that this would subsequently engender a move away from the compliance and blame culture within child protection services and towards a learning culture in which professional judgement and effective relationships with service users improve services to vulnerable children and families. Munro's (2011) challenge is far from being met by leaders and practitioners in the childcare social work field; indeed, this has become even more difficult in light of the cuts by the current government.

Alternative means for children to voice their grievances

Our research demonstrated that IROs were generally more responsive than SWs and SMs to the needs of children in care, as well as showing greater recognition of the need for their voices to be heard. This is consistent with previous research which found that children and young people generally view their IRO positively and that IROs often play an advocacy role, either directly or by referring children to independent advocacy services (Dickens et al, 2014). Despite this, children and young people may not perceive their IRO as having a role in supporting them to make complaints against a LA (Jelicic et al, 2014). Furthermore, there is conflicting evidence about the extent to which IROs fulfil their duty of resolving complaints via formal procedures where necessary. A thematic inspection of ten LAs' IRO services by Ofsted (2013) found that IROs did not consistently understand or utilise formal dispute resolution processes; conversely, Dickens et al (2014) found that complaint escalation procedures were used by most IROs in their study. Nonetheless, despite inconsistencies in extant research, it is reasonable to suggest that for some children in care the loss of the IRO to advocate and speak on their behalf could be keenly felt.

Previous research by Barnes (2009) concluded that independent advocacy services, which are designed to promote the rights of children and young people, can be very helpful in ensuring that the voices (and complaints) of children in care are heard. Indeed, such services can help to 'redress power imbalances' (Braye and Preston-Shoot, 1995, p 139), without which 'changes in the balance of power are unlikely' (Barnes, 2009, p 45). Furthermore, Barnes (2009) highlighted that young people expressed that they would like advocates to assist them in making complaints, expressing their views and challenging decisions made by social services.

However, our study found that the views of children's advocates are not of equal weight to those of other professionals. There are manifold reasons why the views of independent advocates may be discredited by other professionals. Firstly, complaints are often viewed as an attack on organisational or professional security (Oliver and Dalrymple, 2008) and, as such, independent advocates may be 'viewed with suspicion by risk-averse welfare systems' (Parry et al, 2008, p 7). Secondly, advocates may be resented by those SWs who 'view themselves as the rightful and determined professional best able to voice a child's needs' (Parry et al, 2008, p 12). Finally, advocates may be viewed negatively by professionals who are personally implicated in a complaint. Having said this, it has been found that relationships between advocates and other social care professionals can improve over time (Oliver et al, 2006). Thus, in order to ensure that negative attitudes towards independent advocates do not act as a barrier to children's voices being heard, awareness of the advocacy role should be increased among social care professionals (Oliver and Dalrymple, 2008).

Summary

This chapter and our research aimed to explore what happens when the service received by children in care does not meet their needs or when children in care are dissatisfied with the services they are offered. More specifically, this study focused on what happens when children in care face barriers to complaining and how their grievances are perceived and managed by professionals, as well as exploring the alternative means by which children express their views outside of a formal complaints system. Similar to previous research, our study found that – despite the introduction of guidelines and procedures aimed at encouraging and supporting children and young people to complain – children in care are still wary about making complaints about the services they receive (Pithouse and Crowley, 2007; Barnes, 2009). This was found to be the case even when children were aware of the complaint mechanisms available to them. Further barriers for children in care to make complaints were identified within our study, including gatekeeping by professionals, power imbalances and the existence of a 'blame culture'. Given that a complaints mechanism was built into the Children Act 1989, partly to give a formal voice to children who are abused in care, it is concerning that it remains largely unused. As we have seen sexual exploitation of children in care across the country has continued, and, as during the Waterhouse scandal, children's voices have gone unheard and the system has failed to protect them as a result (Waterhouse, 2000; Ofsted, 2014). While a complaint process now exists, as long as children continue to face barriers in using it, it will remain largely ineffective.

8

Summary and conclusions

Summary of key findings

Children's participation in meetings

It appears that the extent to which children and young people participate in their review meetings and decision making more widely has not changed or improved in the last 25 years, despite the introduction of the IRO role in 2002 and the ratification of the UNCRC in 1991. The right to participation is one of the three cornerstones of the Convention, alongside the right to protection and the right to provision. The findings from this research are strikingly similar to the research carried out by Nigel Thomas in 2002.

This research suggests that the CiC reviews and Child Protection Conferences do not encourage meaningful participation by young people or parents. The young participants in this study reported that they had experienced numerous changes of SWs and that this had impacted their ability to trust and develop a meaningful relationship with them. In turn, this impacted on how they engaged with SWs generally, including in key meetings. The relationship with the SW was seen as very important; when young people reported having a poor relationship with their SW, they also felt more negatively about meetings. The young participants said that their relationship with their IRO was much more stable and that this benefited them – although none of the young people had ever met with their IRO between the reviews. Overall, the young participants showed an acute awareness of the time pressures faced by the SWs who worked with them, and some showed a frustration with 'the system'.

Most SWs and SMs demonstrated only a limited understanding of the concept of participation. On the whole, IROs showed a better understanding but were vocal about the lack of suitable training they could attend. Additionally, professionals were only able to give limited examples of how participation was being encouraged, such as through children and young people chairing their own reviews and the use of new technologies, such as mobile phone apps. Most of the SMs – all of whom had had lengthy careers in the sector – said that as far as they were aware, there had been no real improvements in practice in the last 25 years in relation to how effectively CiC reviews engage young people. This is a disappointing finding but one that aligns with previous research.

Most of the examples offered by the professionals interviewed in this study in relation to children's and young people's participation seemed tokenistic when considered in relation to Hart's (1992) 'ladder' of participation. This is exemplified most clearly in the acknowledgement by the professionals that though the views of children and young people were solicited, this would rarely impact on the decisions made. The young participants felt that their views (and the views of their advocates) were not taken as seriously as the views of the professionals who attended their reviews, and the SWs who were interviewed agreed with them on this point.

The majority of the children and young people interviewed in both LAs as part of this study did not feel that their views were taken into account, either during or following reviews. Consequently, many did not see the value in contributing to a process in which matters concerning them had already been predetermined by professionals. Some of the young participants expressed feeling that they had been let down by SWs who did not follow up tasks that were agreed at reviews and that were important to them. Subsequently, this had an impact on the children and young people feeling able to trust the professionals working with them and their engagement in the review.

The young participants, IROs and SWs all appeared to be in agreement that young people did not have any means to input into determining the practicalities of the meeting – for example, where the review would take place, when it would take place, who would be invited and what would be on the agenda. SWs and IROs confirmed that these decisions were taken by the professionals and, in some cases, by the IROs' administrative support staff. This meant that sometimes young people were not invited to their reviews or, on occasion, were not even informed that their reviews were taking place.

There was also an issue in the two LAs where interviews for this study were conducted whereby reviews were scheduled to take place during school hours so as to meet timescales prescribed either by government guidelines or by local policies. This practice caused detriment to children: some were unable to attend the meetings due to the timing or were prevented from doing so, while those who were able to attend could only do so through missing classes, to the disadvantage of their education. The necessity of meeting such timescales appeared to routinely trump the need for children to have the opportunity to attend and meaningfully participate in their review meetings. This was another noteworthy finding, which suggests that Munro's (2012) recommendations in relation to the child protection system have not been implemented in these LAs. The only time when young people had a demonstrable role in determining the outcome of the meeting was when they chaired their own review meetings.

In terms of Child Protection Conferences, most young people had never been invited to a conference and those who had attended one found it to be a negative experience. Parents felt unsupported throughout the child protection process, reporting feelings of powerlessness, intimidation and fear. They said that they found Child Protection Conferences in particular to be stigmatising and oppressive, and this led to them not trusting SWs and often other key agencies. The majority of parents did not find their SWs to be helpful, which could increase the likelihood of disengagement from services. It was interesting to find that some parents said that they felt sorry for their SWs and stated that they seemed stressed and under too much pressure and were not able to deliver on their promises. The parents interviewed as part of this study demonstrated an acute awareness of SWs' high caseloads and the bureaucratic pressures they faced.

Barriers to meaningful participation

From the young participants' perspectives, the main barriers to meaningful participation was their relationship (or lack thereof) with their SWs, the amount of time professionals had to spend with them, and the high turnover of social work staff and the subsequent impact of this on relationship building.

Most of the young participants emphasised the importance of a 'humane' element to their relationships with their SWs and IROs. The examples which were given of good practice may seem unremarkable – instances where a SW or IRO had taken the time with a young person to share a joke or sit down for a cup of tea and a chat – but to the young person this was seen as proof that the professional actually cared about them. This echoed the findings by Selwyn and Riley (2015), where the importance of the relationship between the young person and the professional is emphasised. Some of these exchanges would be difficult to capture in an assessment or case note but they are of doubtless significance to children and young people: there is a sense of the professional communicating with a genuine interest, rather than out of a sense of obligation because they have an assessment to write or a form to complete. One young participant, Kiera, described having a professional who 'talks to me normally'. From the author's perspective, this should be basic social work practice – the norm which children and young people experience, rather than the exception.

In this study, none of the young participants had met with their IROs between the review meetings. IROs stated that they would see children between reviews only if they were going through dispute resolution procedures with the LA, which in itself was very rare. All of the SWs and IROs identified the impact of high caseloads upon their ability to ensure that children and young people were able to participate in their review in a meaningful manner. It was striking that only one of the SMs raised high caseloads as being an issue; this emphasises the disconnect between the views of SMs and all other participants in relation to frontline practice. The majority of the young participants also raised the issue of professionals not having enough time for them. The issues of retention of SWs and high caseloads are ongoing and show no signs of being resolved. A recent study has shown that 92 per cent of SWs are working an average of ten hours' unpaid overtime per week. As a direct result of this, over 50 per cent of current SWs are considering leaving the profession within the next 18 months (Osbourne, 2017).

Another barrier to participation was workers' commitment to the concept of 'meaningful participation' itself: some professionals showed reticence about involving children in matters which they saw as 'adult issues'. Others expressed concerns that through over-involving children in decision-making processes, professionals were preventing them from being 'normal' children. As Bruce (2014, p 515) notes, 'despite the imperatives to involve children, a recurring theme has been the difficulty in achieving a balance between the child's right to have a voice and a duty to protect children and young people'. Sanders and Mace (2006) raise the issue of inappropriate exposure to information and responsibility. In this study, professionals' concerns appeared to be more in relation to the children and young people not knowing what was best for them – a 'paternalistic' attitude – rather than the need to protect them from information.

A further key barrier to young people participating meaningfully in reviews was that on occasion the meetings were used as a means of 'blaming and shaming' them. Archard and Skivenes (2009, p 393) rightly state that 'children should not be intimidated by the circumstances in which they are asked to present their views'. It was problematic, therefore, that all of the IROs and some of the young people in this study reported other professionals – especially school staff and foster carers – using review meetings to 'blame and shame' the young person.

Our research highlighted that despite the introduction of guidelines and procedures which should encourage and support children and young people to complain when they are dissatisfied with the service they are receiving, it is evident that children are still very hesitant about complaining. The young people interviewed for this study expressed feeling that it would make their situation worse, and they perceived complaints against social services as being pointless and/ or too difficult to make. Although it is positive that some of the professionals interviewed for this study demonstrated an understanding of the difficulties faced by children when they wished to complain, the fact that the majority of SMs felt that children were justified in their feelings due to the negative impact it would have on the relationship between them and their SW is troubling. This may be due to the existence of the 'blame culture' in which SWs are fearful of being blamed by a service user when they make a complaint. This, in turn, does not fully place the needs of the child as a priority. These findings were also highlighted by Parry et al (2008) and Dickens et al (2014), indicating that SWs and managers would downplay complaints expressed by children in order to avoid formal procedures. A recurrent theme which became apparent through the interviews was an emphasis on professionals to adhere to timescales and bureaucratic duties, to the detriment of learning from and acting upon complaints.

Some of the young participants articulated an awareness of the constraints of 'the system' and of needing to fight it to make their voice heard. Some were also aware of how bureaucratic pressures meant that their designated professionals did not always have time for them. The SWs and IROs spoke about the difficulties of bureaucracy and how this impacted on how much time they could spend with young people. The picture which emerged was reminiscent of Forrester's (2016) depiction of 'zombie social work', whereby targets and processes are prioritised over real efforts to improve the lives of vulnerable children and families. These LAs appeared to be in a state of defensive practice, relying on technical solutions to complex problems. This is in line with Munro's (2012) view that social work is too focused on 'doing things right when it should be focused on doing the right thing', and suggests that in these LAs very little has improved since Munro made her recommendations in 2012. In addition, the SMs demonstrated only limited curiosity in relation to how to go about addressing the issues in the system.

Improving children's and young people's participation in reviews

There was a clear contradiction between what professionals would say in terms of participation and what they were actually doing in practice. All of the professionals interviewed as part of this study said it was very important that young people could meaningfully participate in decision making and meetings but their ideals were all too often abandoned in practice; instead, they would dictate 'this is what the LA is doing'. It is noteworthy that although SWs emphasised the importance of children's participation, they showed no evidence of even trying to meet the basic elements of participation, such as ensuring children played a role in deciding when and where their review took place. This evidences a disconnect between what SWs think they are doing and what is happening in practice, and is a clear example of wilful blindness (Heffernan, 2014) and espoused theory and theory in use (Argyris and Schön, 1974).

The young participants and professionals involved in this study made various suggestions for improving participation. For the young participants, this generally came down to measures aimed at making them feel more comfortable, for example, making the process feel more like a 'chat', the provision of refreshments at the meeting or them being able to bring a friend to the first review. This research highlighted that when children chaired their own reviews, it had a very positive impact on their engagement in the meeting. While some of the IROs interviewed as part of this study were committed to the principle of providing young people with the opportunity to chair their own meetings, others were not and did not offer young people this option. This lack of consistency is an issue which requires consideration in this LA. The practice of young people chairing their own reviews has not been researched previously; given that this study has highlighted that it can improve children's participation, it would benefit from further exploration across a range of LAs.

Child Protection Conferences

The research outlined in this book – like much other research – found that young people's and in particular parent's views of Child Protection Conferences was very negative. There is a real concern that at a critical point in the building of trusting relationships between professionals and families, Child Protection Conferences put a considerable strain on parents and they feel blamed and shamed by the process. Most of the children we interviewed were not clear about the purpose of a

Child Protection Conference and their participation was minimal. Both children and parents from our study described Child Protection Conferences as a negative experience, with most parents viewing them as 'stigmatising' and part of a 'blame game'.

Half of the children we interviewed appeared to view social work involvement in a positive light and felt that their SW had helped improve things in their lives. This is a positive finding, particularly when one considers that the interviews were carried out with children who were on a Child Protection Plan – a time when, typically, relations between families and SWs are fraught. Although most parents did not take the same view as their children, a small number of parents were appreciative of the help they had received from children's services. However, the majority of the parents interviewed were very negative about their experiences of both SWs and Child Protection Conferences, and the high turnover of SWs was cited as being a particular problem in terms of relationship building and trust for both children and parents.

The Children Act 1989, the Children Act 2004 and Munro's report (2011) highlight the importance of engaging children and young people in the child protection system to ensure their voices are heard, yet this does not seem to be happening. According to this research, children and young people are rarely attending conferences, and when they do, they do not feel listened to or supported and have only minimal or partial understanding of the process.

Children and parents need to be better informed regarding the process of Child Protection Conferences, and information needs to be provided in an accessible format. The process needs to be explained in a clear way, with reports and assessments tailored to each individual and shared in advance of the conference. Child Protection Chairs need to meet with parents and young people prior to the conference to ensure they understand the purpose of such meetings and to allow their views to be shared. SWs need to be supportive throughout the process and take the time to explain both the purpose of meetings and reports and also how they think the process will help improve things for children and parents. At a policy level, it would be wise for the government to consider whether Child Protection Conferences are actually fit for purpose. A casual observer might reasonably conclude that there are better ways of engaging parents and children which are less likely to foster in parents' feelings of blame and shame. One such solution might be the wider use of family group conferences – meetings which are led by the family.

Substantive insights

Despite the plethora of legislative, policy and guidance frameworks that exist to promote the involvement of children in decision making, as detailed in the literature review, the existing research paints a very bleak picture (Thomas and O'Kane, 1999; Thomas, 2011; Barnes, 2012; Ofsted, 2013; Pert et al, 2014). Previous studies have outlined that children and young people felt dissatisfied with the levels of participation offered to them. This study supports this viewpoint: examples where children and young people were able to participate were found to be limited and often perfunctory.

Taking reviews as a process and not a single event (Sinclair, 1998; DfES, 2010; Thomas, 2011), children and young people reported being offered little opportunity at any stage to input their views. This was most acutely felt in the planning and preparation stages of the review process. Young people, IROs and SWs all agreed that young people had little to no control over who would be invited to the review, when it would be held and where it would be held. It was only the more confident children or young people who seemed to be able to exercise some control over the process. The feeling of a lack of control has significant implications for children's and young people's self-confidence (Bostock, 2005). It is imperative that professionals try to promote the self-determination of an already-vulnerable group (The College of Social Work, 2013). Better preparation of children and young people before their reviews is clearly necessary (Sinclair, 1998; Roesch-March et al, 2016), and more emphasis should be placed upon SWs and IROs regarding this to ensure that it happens. None of the young participants reported having met their IRO between reviews and they were only given a brief chance before each review to consider, with the IRO, any issues they wanted to discuss at the review. This supports the findings of previous studies, that children did not feel adequately prepared or consulted for reviews (Thomas and O'Kane, 1999; Munro, 2001).

This research, in line with previous studies, found that the relationship between child and SW is key to ensuring that meaningful participation occurs (Thomas and O'Kane, 1999). The main barriers highlighted by SWs, IROs and the young participants were high caseloads, an overly bureaucratic system and IROs not meeting with children regularly enough. Subsequently, this meant that children did not feel adequately involved and felt as though their views were side-lined. Thomas (2011) reported that a common theme was children feeling disillusioned with the review process and that their views are not listened to. Similarly, Munro (2001, p 135) stated: 'most report that the purpose of the meeting is to talk about, rather than to, them'. This study has confirmed these findings and found that children generally held negative views of the review process.

It was noteworthy that the SMs and IROs in this study did not appear to be leading the way in terms of children's participation. There was no clear vision presented; SMs seemed to lack curiosity about what was happening in frontline practice. There was limited evidence of the impact of Munro's (2012) review of the child protection system in relation to trying to make social work less process-driven and less focused on bureaucracy. The following observation by Forrester seems pertinent to the situation in the two LAs in which we carried out this research:

> There is lots of attention paid to the management of the service with very little sense of a shared understanding of what the service is actually for. Without this the attempts to manage the system become weirdly empty. Much time and effort is devoted to activities that do not seem to have a clear purpose or likely impact. (Forrester, 2016)

This ties in with IROs describing reviews as 'another crisis meeting' and of having to 'wing it' at times, rather than the meeting being properly planned. According to one SM the central purpose of the review – to review the care plan – was not taking place due to SWs failing to ensure that this document was up to date. Reviewing the care plan is the key objective of the review, as mandated by policy and legislation; the fact that this core element of the review did not appear to be taking place was deeply concerning.

These findings correspond with earlier studies, which suggests that some of the key themes drawn out by this study may well be characteristic of practices beyond these specific LAs. If one considers recent research such as the Care Crisis Review (2018), Forrester (2016), Shoesmith (2016) and Featherstone et al (2014), a pattern can be seen to emerge, with which the findings of this study correspond. This pattern suggests that a combination of austerity, the modernisation agenda, a paternalistic approach taken by professionals, New Public Management (NPM) and systemic issues in social work have all had a cumulative impact on the quality of practice by SWs in relation to children in care. The complexities SWs, IROs and SMs face in the current climate should not be minimised. The operation of a seemingly all-powerful inspectorate, Ofsted (whereby a poor inspection often leads to SMs losing their jobs), may also lead to this situation being all the more challenging for those who are trying to improve the lives for children in care.

One of the key findings from this study was the lack of understanding that professionals had about children's participation. Although they considered participation by children and young people to be important, their statements were usually qualified in some way and the practice examples which were given were often tokenistic. It would therefore seem beneficial for professionals to receive training about why meaningful participation is important, for example, in relation to increasing confidence and empowerment of children and young people, and ideas about how it can be implemented. Such training would ideally involve children and young people who have either been in care or are currently in care. It could also provide a forum for discussion and formulation of a policy and vision in relation to meaningful participation of children and young people in reviews. This would hopefully help move practice from an obsession with 'what' and 'when' to a focus on 'how' and 'why' (Forrester, 2016). It is particularly important that there is a review of the training that IROs receive on a national basis, particularly in relation to participation, as IROs and SWs need further support in this vital area of practice.

Given that the IRO workforce is reasonably consistent (and certainly more so than that of SWs), IROs should aim to visit children and young people at least once between reviews so that this relationship can be improved. It is noted that while this recommendation is in line with current policy (DfES, 2010), it is not something that is being put into practice in this particular LA. One of the benefits of the IRO visiting between reviews would be that it provides the opportunity to discuss the review agenda with the child or young person. It would make sense for this visit to take place about one month prior to the review date. The IRO and child or young person would then be able to decide together who was going to be invited to the review, the time it would occur, the location, any refreshments which might need to be provided and whether a 'split review' would be required. This pre-review meeting would give the child or young person much greater ownership over their review from the very start. The IRO would also be able to discuss with the child or young person about the option of chairing their meeting. When we consider some of the language used by the professionals in this study LA – 'this is what the LA is doing'; 'I know the case better'; 'our system' – the impression is very much that the LA 'owns' the review at the moment, rather than the young person.

One idea is for a training day for children and young people about CiC reviews, covering issues such as why their review is important and how they can participate, which could be offered to all children and young people within six months of coming into care. This event could be led by young people who have chaired their own meetings. It could help to educate children and young people about how to chair a review and provide them with a menu of choices regarding how they can participate, including using new technologies such as the MOMO app.[1]

Given that the SMs who were interviewed appeared somewhat detached from frontline practice, it is recommended that they should attend a review meeting at least once a year and shadow a SW and an IRO at least twice a year. It is noted that when SMs are able to display greater knowledge and oversight of what is happening on the ground, this is recognised and praised by Ofsted (2017) in LAs which are considered to be Outstanding.

The structural and systemic reforms which were outlined in the Munro (2012) review of the child protection system have had a decidedly limited impact on the social work practice in these LAs. The reforms suggested by Munro (2012) are sound and evidence-based and this research further highlights why such systemic changes are necessary. The technical rationale approach pervaded social work practice in these LAs and led to SWs spending too much of their time fulfilling bureaucratic processes rather than getting to know the children and young people they are working with and supporting them to improve their lives. In order for this to change, a change in culture is required within these LAs. Shortly before I carried out this particular field work, a piece of research in one of the LAs concluded that SWs spent 80 per cent of their time in front of a computer and that 70 per cent of the data that SWs filled out on the LA Integrated Children's System (ICS) forms will have already been inputted in other parts of the system. Until the bureaucratic elements of the role are streamlined and reduced, SWs will not have the time to concentrate on relationship building with the children and families they are working with. If such changes are made, the morale of SWs should improve as it will enable them to see the value of the work that they are doing. Munro eloquently reinforces this point:

> Social work with child protection used to be the elite part of social work. Back in the 1980s and 90s it was very difficult to get a job in child protection because when people got one they stayed there. The teams around London

would've been full of people who had been in post for years and years.

That demoralisation of the staff is a direct response to managerialism not recognising the nature of the work that you need to do with families. To me, the need to challenge the work conditions that we need is one of the important tasks ahead. To get a very strong narrative on why we need to have these supports. That they are not because you're fluffy and silly and need extra care, it's because you're doing more challenging work. (Munro, 2016, p 14)

Finding strategies to improve the retention of SWs and the appeal of a career in child protection social work is essential, both within these LAs and nationally. SWs need to enjoy, as far as possible, the work that they are doing rather than feeling as though they are rushing from one crisis to another, and with an ever-present anxiety that they will be blamed if a tragedy occurs.

A noteworthy finding from this research was that SWs and IROs caseloads were found to be very high – at around 85 for a full-time worker – and SWs and IROs often appeared to be overwhelmed by the sheer amount and complexity of their work. This would suggest that there needs to be further investment in SWs and IROs in these LAs, as the evidence is clear that when caseloads are lower, the standard of social work practice is better and more likely to be child-focused (Diaz and Drewery, 2016; Ofsted, 2017). For IROs to fulfil the functions recommended, particularly in relation to visiting children and young people between reviews, the caseloads should be around 50 for a full-time worker, with an absolute maximum of 70. For SWs to realistically be able to fulfil both the family support and relationship-building functions of their role and the bureaucratic requirements, their caseloads should be no higher than 15. This type of caseload has played a key role in LAs such as Essex achieving a 'Good' rating from Ofsted.

Professionals should be encouraged to make reviews more enjoyable for children and young people. As well as the difficult subjects that may need to be discussed, it should be remembered that reviews can also be an opportune moment to celebrate the child's or young person's achievements. Reviews need to become less formal and more strengths-based, so that children and young people feel encouraged and want to participate. This could involve carrying out an activity or game during the review and/or food being made available for attendees, which young people help to choose. In this sense, much could be learned from family group conferences, which are much better at ensuring meaningful participation by young people than Child Protection Conferences and CiC reviews are presently (Brown, 2007).

Theoretically, IROs are independent from the LA. However there has been mounting dismay at the lack of independence of some IROs (Tickle, 2016). In a 2014 judgment, Mr Justice Holman said: 'The whole point and purpose of the system and machinery of independent reviewing officers is precisely to keep the local authority (who are no doubt extraordinarily busy and overworked) on their toes and to be asking awkward questions' (Tickle, 2016). This creates tension, particularly as most IROs are directly employed by the LA.

The debate about the usefulness and necessity of the IRO role has heightened following the government's national fostering stocktake report published in February 2018. One of the 36 recommendations was that LAs should have the option to remove the IRO role and use those savings to invest in the frontline:

> The real issue is whether, rather than spending large amounts of money checking that children are being appropriately placed and cared for in the case system we should invest that money in more frontline and line management staff to make that happen. ... Our conclusion is that, despite the commendable commitment of some individuals, we saw little to recommend the IRO role. (Narey and Owers, 2018)

This recommendation has been strongly criticised by the British Association of Social Work (BASW), the National Association of Independent Reviewing Officers (NAIRO) and the Children's Commissioner (Stevenson, 2018). One favourable aspect that the IRO role has generally brought to children in care is stability; in previous research, the turnover of IROs has been noted to be low (Dickens et al, 2015). My research would suggest that given the current challenges in terms of retention and high turnover of SWs, the IROs provide a degree of consistency to young people, and as such, it would be deeply troubling if the government decided to get rid of the role.

A new and important finding that this study has highlighted is the suggestion that reviews are sometimes being used to 'blame and shame' children and young people or as an opportunity to pit professionals against each other, with IROs calling into question the competence of SWs. It would be beneficial to determine whether this is an endemic issue across the system nationally or whether this is just isolated to the

LAs where I undertook my research. It is noteworthy that shortly after this study had been carried out, one of the LAs received a 'Requiring Improvement' rating by Ofsted in relation to children in care – the average rating across LAs – while the other LA received a 'Good' overall rating, suggesting that poor practice in this area may not be limited to this particular LA.

Final conclusions

This study has provided an insight into the views and perceptions of young people and professionals involved in key decision-making forums. Child Protection Conferences and CiC reviews are key meetings that make major decisions about children's and parents' lives and it is only by involving parents and children more meaningfully in this process that we will improve practice with families.

The importance of involving parents, children and young people in decisions that affect them has gained momentum over the last 30 years. Despite this, there has been limited research where children, young people and their parents have been asked directly about their experiences. The young participants' perceptions have been compared with the professionals who are involved in delivering the service. This gives an insight into how those who deliver services may see things differently to those who are in receipt of them.

The study found that the young participants had a better understanding than SMs of the challenges faced by SWs in offering them the service that they deserved and required. For example, the young participants were aware of the time pressures faced by the professionals working with them and knew that this impacted on the care provided to them. A significant and worrying finding was the apparent disconnect between what SMs thought was happening on the frontline, the potential reality experienced by the young participants and the views of the IROs and SWs.

The bureaucratic elements of the SW and IRO roles were noted to frequently take precedence over what would be in the best interests of the child or young person. Review meetings sometimes became 'crisis meetings' or were held to fit statutory timescales rather than at a time which was convenient for the child or young person. SMs appeared to prioritise the bureaucratic features of the role.

There was a clear disconnect between the espoused theory of SWs, IROs and SMs and the theory in use. Professionals suggested that participation was important but in practice they did not involve children and young people in decisions such as when the review would take place, where it would take place, what would be on the agenda or who would be invited. When there were contentious issues at play, the young participants were aware that their view carried less weight, while the professionals confirmed that they felt that certain decisions could only be made by the professionals involved.

Where children or young people had chaired their own review, participation was much improved. In these circumstances the young participants felt that they had far greater ownership over the process. Evidently, there are manifold complicating factors in respect of this practice that require consideration and, of course, it will not be right for every child; however, chairing their review is one means by which to ensure that the child, as a person, is more authentically involved in the decisions about their life. At the very least, it is essential that young people play a role in deciding when and where the review is going to take place, what is on the agenda and who is going to be invited to the meeting.

Note

[1]   The MOMO self-advocacy app allows children and young people to express their views using an online questionnaire.

References

A and S v Lancashire County Council (2012) EWHC Fam 1689.

Adams, R., Dominelli, L. and Payne, M. (2009) *Critical Practice in Social Work* (2nd edn), London: Palgrave Macmillan.

ADCS (Association of Directors of Children's Services) (2016) 'North west region update April 2016', available from: http://adcs.org.uk/general-subject/article/north-west-region-update-april-2016 [Accessed 26 January 2018].

Anderson, J., Funk, J., Elliott, R. and Hull Smith, P. (2003) 'Parental support and pressure and children's extracurricular activities: relationships with amount of involvement and affective experience of participation', *Journal of Applied Developmental Psychology*, 24(2): 241–57.

Appleton, J.V. (2015) 'Working alongside one another', *Child Abuse Review*, 24(5): 116–29.

Archard, D. and Skivenes, M. (2009) 'Hearing the child', *Child & Family Social Work*, 14(4): 391–9.

Argyris, C. and Schön, D. (1974) *Theory in Practice: Increasing Professional Effectiveness*, San Francisco, CA: Jossey-Bass.

Arnstein, S.R. (1969) 'A ladder of citizen participation', *Journal of the American Institute of Planners*, 35(4): 216–24.

Ashley, C. and Nixon, P. (2007) *Family Group Conferences: Where Next? Policies and Practices for the Future*, London: Family Rights Group.

Babbie, E. (2004) *The Practice of Social Research* (10th edn), Belmont: Wadsworth.

Baginsky, M. (2013) 'Retaining experienced social workers in children's services: the challenge facing local authorities in England', London: Department for Education.

Barnes, K.V. (2009) 'Caring for rights: social work and advocacy with looked after children and young people', Doctoral dissertation, University of Warwick.

Barnes, V. (2012) 'Social work and advocacy with young people: rights and care in practice', *The British Journal of Social Work*, 42(7): 1275–92.

BASW (British Association of Social Work) (2012) *Code of Ethics*.

BASW (British Association of Social Work) (2015) 'The Code of Ethics for Social Work', available from: http://cdn.basw.co.uk/upload/basw_112315-7.pdf [Accessed 15 November 2017].

BASW (British Association of Social Work) (2018) *Code of Ethics for Social Work*, Birmingham: BASW.

Becker, G. (1971) *The Economics of Discrimination*, Chicago: University of Chicago Press.

Bell, M. (1999) 'Working in partnership in child protection: the conflicts', *The British Journal of Social Work*, 29(3): 437–55.

Bell, M. (2002) 'Promoting children's rights through the use of relationship', *Child & Family Social Work*, 7(1): 1–11.

Bennis, W. (2009) *On Becoming a Leader*, San Francisco, CA: Basic Books.

Berridge, D., Bell, K., Sebba, J. and Luke, N. (2015) *The Educational Progress of Looked After Children in England: Technical Report 3: Perspectives of Young People, Social Workers, Carers and Teachers*, Bristol: Nuffield Foundation.

Bessell, S. and Gal, T. (2009) 'Forming partnerships: the human rights of children in need of care and protection', *International Journal of Child Rights*, 17: 283–98.

Best, A. and Andreasen, A. (1977) 'Consumer response to unsatisfactory purchases: a survey of perceiving defects, voicing complaints and obtaining redress', *Law and Society Review*, 11: 701–42.

Bostock, L. (2005) 'Improving the lives of fostered children and young people', *CC Inform*, available from: http://www.ccinform.co.uk/articles.aspx?liArticleID254 [Accessed 15 November 2017].

Bowyer, S. and Roe, A. (2015) *Social Work Recruitment and Retention*, Dartington: Research in Practice.

Boylan, J. and Dalrymple, J. (2009) *Understanding Advocacy for Children and Young People*, London: McGraw-Hill Education (UK).

Boylan, J. and Dalrymple, J. (2011) 'Advocacy, social justice and children's rights, practice', *Practice*, 23(1): 19–30.

Brady, L. (2011) 'Where is my advocate? A scoping report on advocacy services for children and young people in England', *Office of the Children's Commissioner*, 3 January, available from: https://www.childrenscommissioner.gov.uk/wpcontent/uploads/2017/07/A_scoping_report_on_advocacy_services_for_children_and_young_people_in_England.pdf [Accessed 10 February 2020].

Braun, V. and Clarke, V. (2006) 'Using thematic analysis in psychology', *Qualitative Research in Psychology*, 3(2): 77–101.

Braye, S. and Preston-Shoot, M. (1995) *Empowering Practice in Social Care*, Buckingham: Open University Press.

Broadhurst, K., Wastell, D., White, S., Hall, C., Peckover, S., Thompson, K., Pithouse, A. and Davey, D. (2009) 'Performing "initial assessment": identifying the latent conditions for error at the front-door in local authority children's services', *British Journal of Social Work*, 40(2): 352–70.

Brown, L. (2007) 'The adoption and implementation of a service innovation in a social work setting – a case study of family group conferencing in the UK', *Social Policy and Society*, 6(3): 321–32.

Bruce, M. (2014) 'The voice of the child in child protection: whose voice?', *Social Sciences*, 3(3): 514–26, doi: 10.3390/socsci3030514 [Accessed 2 January 2018].

Burgess, C., Daniel, B., Whitfield, E., Derbyshire, D. and Taylor, J. (2013) *Action on Neglect – A Resource Pack*, London: Action for Children.

Butler-Sloss, E. (1988) *Report of the Inquiry into Child Abuse in Cleveland 1987*, London: HMSO.

Bywaters, P. and Brady, G. (2017) *Identifying and Understanding Inequalities in Child Welfare Interventions: Comparative Studies in Four UK Countries. April 2015–March 2017*, Coventry: Nuffield Foundation and University of Coventry.

Care Crisis Review (2018) *Options for Change*, London: Family Rights Group

Carmel, S. (1988) 'Hospital patients' responses to dissatisfaction', *Sociology of Health & Illness*, 10: 262–81.

Carpenter, J.S.W., Webb, C.M. and Bostock, L. (2013) 'The surprisingly weak evidence base for supervision: findings from a system review of research in child welfare practice (2000-2012)', *Children and Youth Services Review*, 35(11): 1843–53.

Cashmore, J. (2002) 'Promoting the participation of children and young people in care', *Child Abuse and Neglect*, 26: 837–47.

Centre for Social Justice (2007) 'Breakthrough Britain', available from: http://www.centreforsocialjustice.org.uk/publications/breakthrough-britain-chairmans-overview [Accessed 27 September 2017].

Children's Commissioner (2019) 'Advocacy for children: children and young people's advocacy in England', 1 December, available from: https://www.childrenscommissioner.gov.uk/wp-content/uploads/2019/06/CCO-Advocacy-for-children-June-2019.pdf [Accessed 10 February 2020].

Clarke, J., Gewirtz, S., Hughes, G. and Humphrey, J. (2000) 'Guarding the public interest? Auditing public services', in J. Clarke, S. Gewirtz and E. McLaughlin (eds) *New Managerialism, New Welfare?* London: Sage, pp 52–70.

Cleaver, H., Nicholson, D., Tarr, S. and Cleaver, D. (2007) *Child Protection, Domestic Violence and Parental Substance Misuse: Family Experiences and Effective Practice*, London: Jessica Kingsley Publishers.

Cleaver, H. and Walker, S. with Meadows, P. (2004) *Assessing Children's Needs and Circumstances: The Impact of the Assessment Framework*, London: Jessica Kingsley Publishers.

College of Social Work (2013) 'Code of ethics', available from: http://www.tcsw.org.uk/uploadedFiles/TheCollege/Members_area/CodeofEthicsAug2013.pdf [Accessed 1 November 2017].

Community Care (2015) Survey, available from: http://www.communitycare.co.uk/2014/06/15/call-action-work-life-balance-survey-reveals-pressure-social-work-places-practitioners-home-lives/ [Accessed 10 March 2018].

Corby, B., Millar, M. and Young, L. (1996) 'Parental participation in child protection work: rethinking the rhetoric', *The British Journal of Social Work*, 26(4): 475–92.

Cossar, J., Brandon, M. and Jordan, P. (2011) *'Don't Make Assumptions': Children's and Young People's Views of the Child Protection System and Messages for Change*, Norwich: Office of the Children's Commissioner, CRCF.

Cossar, J., Brandon, M. and Jordan, P. (2016). 'You've got to trust her and she's got to trust you': Children's views on participation in the child protection system. *Child & Family Social Work*, 21(1): 103–12. https://doi.org/10.1111/cfs.12115

Cowan, D.S. and Halliday, S. (2003) *The Appeal of Internal Review: Law, Administrative Justice, and the (non-) Emergence of Disputes*, London: Hart.

Cowden, M. (2012) 'Capacity, claims and children's rights', *Contemporary Political Theory*, 11: 362–80, available from: http://www.palgrave-journals.com/cpt/journal/v11/n4/abs/cpt201143a.html [Accessed 3 November 2017].

Croft, S. and Beresford, P. (1992) 'The politics of participation', *Critical Social Policy*, 12(35): 20–44.

Dalrymple, J. (2004) 'Developing the concept of professional advocacy: an examination of the role of child and youth advocates in England and Wales', *Journal of Social Work*, 4(2): 179–97.

Denzin, N. K. and Lincoln, Y. S. (2011) *The SAGE Handbook of Qualitative Research*, Thousand Oaks, CA: Sage.

DfE (Department for Education) (2013a) *Positive for Youth: Progress Since December 2011*, London: HMSO.

DfE (Department for Education) (2013b) *Working Together to Safeguard Children: A Guide to Inter-agency Working to Safeguard and Promote the Welfare of Children*, London: HMSO.

DfE (Department for Education) (2014) *Statistics SSDA903 Return Guidance Notes: Children Looked After by Local Authorities in England*, London: HMSO.

DfE (Department for Education) (2016) 'National statistics: children looked after in England including adoption: 2015 to 2016', available from: https://www.gov.uk/government/statistics/children-looked-after-in-england-including-adoption-2015-to-2016 [Accessed 8 November 2017].

DfE (Department for Education) (2018) *Working Together to Safeguard Children: A Guide to Inter-agency Working to Safeguard and Promote the Welfare of Children*, London: HMSO.

DfES (Department for Education and Skills) (2004) *Getting the Best from Complaints: Consultation on the Changes to the Social Services Complaints Procedures for Children, Young People and Other People Making a Complaint*, London: HMSO.

DfES (Department for Education and Skills) (2010) *IRO Handbook: Statutory Guidance for Independent Reviewing Officers and Local Authorities on their Functions in Relation to Case Management and Review for Looked after Children*, London: HMSO.

Diaz, C. and Drewery, S. (2016) 'A critical assessment of evidence-based policy and practice in social work', *Journal of Evidence-Informed Social Work*, 13(4): 425–31.

Diaz, C., Pert, H. and Thomas, N. (2018) '"Just another person in the room": young people's views on their participation in Child in Care Reviews', *Adoption and Fostering*, 42(4): 369–83.

Dickens, J., Schofield, G., Beckett, C., Philip, G. and Young J. (2014) *Care Planning and the Role of the Independent Reviewing Officer: Research Briefing*, Norwich: University of East Anglia.

Dickens, J., Schofield, G., Beckett, C., Philip, G. and Young, J. (2015) *Care Planning and the Role of the Independent Reviewing Officer Report*, Norwich: Centre for Research on Children and Families, University of East Anglia.

DoH (Department of Health) (1989) *The Care of Children: Principles and Practice in Regulations and Guidance*, London: HMSO.

Donaldson, L. J. and Cavanagh, J. (1992) 'Clinical complaints and their handling: a time for change?', *Quality and Safety in Health Care*, 1, 21–5.

Duncalf, Z. (2010) 'Listen Up! Adult care leavers speak out. the views of 310 care leavers aged 17–78', available from: https://strathprints.strath.ac.uk/27410/5/strathprints027410.pdf [Accessed 10 February 2020].

Earle, F., Fox, J., Webb, C. and Bowyer, S. (2017) *Reflective Supervision: Resource Pack*, Dartington: Research in Practice.

Edwards, D. and Parkinson, K. (eds) (2018) *Family Group Conferences in Social Work: Involving Families in Social Care Decision Making*, Bristol: Policy Press.

Fabricant, M.B. and Burghardt, S. (1992) *The Welfare State and Transformation of Social Service Work*, New York and London: M.E. Sharpe.

Faller, K.C. (ed) (1981) *Social Work with Abused and Neglected Children: A Manual of Interdisciplinary Practice*, New York: Simon & Schuster.

Farmer, E. (2014) 'Achieving permanence for children returned to their parents', in T. Rahilly and E. Hendry (eds) *Promoting the Wellbeing of Children in Care: Messages from Research*, London: NSPCC, pp 217–38.

Farnfield, S. (1998) 'The rights and wrongs of social work with children', in J. Cheetham and M. Kazi (eds) *The Working of Social Work*, London: Jessica Kingsley, pp 22–41.

Featherstone, B., Gupta, A., Morris, K. and Warner, J. (2018) 'Let's stop feeding the risk monster: towards a social model of "child protection"', *Families, Relationships and Societies*, 7(1): 7–22.

Featherstone, B., White, S. and Morris, K. (2014) *Re-imagining Child Protection: Towards Humane Social Work with Families*, Bristol: Policy Press.

Foot, C., Gilburt, H., Dunn, P., Jabbal, J., Seale, B., Goodrich, J. and Taylor, J. (2014) *People in Control of Their Own Health and Care*, London: The King's Fund.

Forrester, D. (2008) 'Is the care system failing children?', *The Political Quarterly*, 79(2): 206–11.

Forrester, D. (2016) 'What, when, why and how: zombie social work and the need for a new narrative', in E. Solomon (ed) *Rethinking Children's Services: Fit for the Future?*, London: Catch 22 and National Children's Bureau, pp 8–14.

Forrester, D., Goodman, K., Cocker, C., Binnie, C. and Jensch, G. (2009) 'What is the impact of care on children's welfare? Review of research findings from England and Wales and their policy implications', *Journal of Social Policy*, 38(3): 439–56.

Fylkesnes, M.K., Taylor, J. and Iversen, A.C. (2018) 'Precarious participation: exploring ethnic minority youth's narratives about out-of-home placement in Norway', *Children and Youth Services Review*, 88: 341–7.

Geer, B. (1964) 'First days in the field', in P. Hammond (ed) *Sociologists at Work*, Garden City, NY: Doubleday.

George, M., Graham, C. and Lennard, L. (2007) *Complaint Handling: Principles and Best Practice*, Leicester: Centre for Utility Consumer Law, University of Leicester.

Gibbs, J., Dwyer, J. and Vivekandanda, K. (2009) 'Leading practice: a resource guide for child protection frontline and middle managers', Melbourne: Victorian Government of Human Resources.

Gilligan, R. (2004) 'Promoting resilience in child and family social work: issues for social work practice, education and policy', *Social Work Education*, 23(1): 93–104.

Godar, R. (2015) 'The hallmarks of effective participation: evidencing the voice of the child', in M. Ivory (ed), *The Voice of the Child: Evidence Review*, Dartington: Research in Practice, pp 10–21.

Goodman-Delahunty, J., Verbrugge, H. and Taitz, M. (2013) 'Complaining to the police: insights from a psychological analysis', *Policing: A Journal of Policy and Practice*, 7: 280–8. http://doi.org/10.1093/police/pat016

Hale, B. (2006) 'Understanding children's rights: theory and practice', *Family Court Review*, 44(3): 350–60.

Hall, C. and Slembrouck, S. (2001) 'Parent participation in social work meetings – the case of child protection conferences', *European Journal of Social Work*, 4(2): 143–60.

Hallett, C. (2000) 'Ahead of the game or behind the times? The Scottish children's hearings system in international context', *International Journal of Law, Policy and the Family*, 14(1): 31–44, https://doi.org/10.1093/lawfam/14.1.31

Hanna, N. (1992) 'The time limit hurdle: ruling out patients complaints', *New Law Journal*, 31: 1098–1100.

Hart, R. (1992) *Children's Participation from Tokenism to Citizenship*, Florence: UNICEF Innocenti Research Centre.

Hartas, D. and Lindsay, G. (2011) 'Young people's involvement in service evaluation and decision making', *Emotional and Behavioural Difficulties*, 16(2): 129–43.

Havlicek, J., Curry, A. and Villalpando, F. (2018) 'Youth participation in foster youth advisory boards: perspectives of facilitators', *Children and Youth Services Review*, 84: 255–70.

Healy, K. and Darlington, Y. (2009) 'Service user participation in diverse child protection contexts: principles for practice', *Child & Family Social Work*, 14(4): 420–30.

Heffernan, M. (2014) *Wilful Blindness: Why We Ignore the Obvious at Our Peril*, London: Walker & Company.

Higgs, L. (2011) 'Exclusive survey: youth services and children's services worst hit as cuts average 13 per cent', in *Children and Young People Now*, 25 January, pp 6–7.

Hill, M. (2006) Children's voices on ways of having a voice: children's and young people's perspectives on methods used in research and consultation', *Childhood*, 13(1): 69–89.

Hirschman, A. (1970) *Exit, Voice and Loyalty: Responses to Decline in Firms, Organizations and States*, Cambridge, MA: Harvard University Press.

Holland, S., Renold, E., Ross, N.J. and Hillman, A. (2010) 'Power, agency and participatory agendas: a critical exploration of young people's engagement in participative qualitative research', *Childhood* 17(3): 360–75.

Holmes, L. and McDermid, S. (2013) 'How social workers spend their time in frontline children's social care in England', *Journal of Children's Services*, 8(2): 123–33.

Hood, R., Goldacre, A., Grant, R. and Jones, R. (2016) 'Exploring demand and provision in English child protection services', *British Journal of Social Work*, 46(4), 923–41. doi:10.1093/bjsw/bcw044.

Howe, D. (2006) 'Disabled children, parent–child interaction and attachment', *Child & Family Social Work*, 11: 95–106.

Howe, D. (2014) *The Complete Social Worker*, Basingstoke: Palgrave Macmillan.

Jelicic, H., Hart, D., La Valle, R., Fauth, R., Gill, C. and Straw, C. (2014) *The Role of Independent Reviewing Officers (IROs) in England: Final Report*, London: NCB.

Keegan Eamon, M. and Kopels, S. L. (2004) ' "For reasons of poverty": Court challenges to child welfare practices and mandated programs', *Children and Youth Services Review*, 26(9): 821–36. https://doi.org/10.1016/j.childyouth.2004.02.023.

Kennan, D., Brady, B. and Forkan, C. (2016) *Exploring the Effectiveness of Structures and Procedures Intended to Support Children's Participation in Child Welfare, Child Protection and Alternative Care Services: A Systematic Literature Review*, Galway: The UNESCO Child and Family Research Centre, the National University of Ireland, Galway.

Križ, K. and Skivenes, M. (2017) 'Child welfare workers' perceptions of children's participation: a comparative study of England, Norway and the USA (California)', *Child & Family Social Work*, 22(15): 11–22.

Lancaster, Y.P. (2007) 'Listening to young children: respecting the voice of the child', in G. Pugh and B. Duffy (eds) *Contemporary Issues in the Early Years*, London: Sage, pp 63–75.

Lancaster, Y.P. (2010) 'Listening to young children: enabling children to be seen and heard', in G. Pugh and B. Duffy (eds) *Contemporary Issues in the Early Years*, London: Sage, pp 79–94.

Larkins, C., Kiili, J. and Palsanen, K. (2014) 'A lattice of participation: reflecting on examples of children's and young people's collective engagement in influencing social welfare policies and practices', *European Journal of Social Work*, 17(5): 718–36.

Leigh, J. (2017) *Blame, Culture and Child Protection*, London: Palgrave Macmillan.

Leviner, P. (2018) 'Child participation in the Swedish child protection system: child-friendly focus but limited child influence on outcomes', *The International Journal of Children's Rights*, 26(1): 136–58.

Levy, A. and Kahan, B. (1991) *The Pindown Experience and the Protection of Children: The Report of the Staffordshire Child Care Inquiry 1990*, Staffordshire County Council.

Lindsey, D. (1992) 'Reliability of the foster care placement decision: a review', *Research on Social Work Practice*, 2(1): 65–80.

Lipsky, M. (1980) *Street-Level Bureaucracy: Dilemmas of the Individual in Public Services*, New York: Russell Sage Foundation.

Local Government Ombudsman (2009) *Guidance on Running a Complaints System: Guidance on Good Practice*. Online [Accessed September 2018].

Lowden, J. (2002) 'Children's rights: a decade of dispute', *Journal of Advanced Nursing*, 37: 100–7.

Luke, N., Sinclair, I., Woolgar, M. and Sebba, J. (2014) 'What works in preventing and treating poor mental health in looked after children?' NSPCC/Rees Centre.

MacNaughton, G., Hughes, P. and Smith, K. (2007) 'Young children's rights and public policy: practices and possibilities for citizenship in the early years', *Children & Society*, 21: 458–69.

Malone, K. and Hartung, C. (2010) 'Challenges of participatory practice with children', in B. Percy-Smith and N. Thomas (eds) *A Handbook of Children and Young People's Participation: Perspectives from theory and practice*, Abingdon: Routledge, pp 24–39.

Mannay, D. (2016) *Visual, Narrative and Creative Research Methods: Application, Reflection and Ethics*, Abingdon: Routledge.

Mannay, D., Evans, R., Staples, E., Hallett, S., Roberts, L. Rees, A. and Andrews, D. (2017) 'The consequences of being labeled "looked-after": exploring the educational experiences of looked-after children and young people in Wales', *British Educational Research Journal*, 43(4): 683–99.

Marsh, P. and Crow, G. (1998) *Family Group Conferences in Child Welfare*, Oxford: Blackwell Science.

McDowall, J. (2016) 'Are we listening? The need to facilitate participation in decision-making by children and young people in out-of-home care', *Developing Practice: The Child, Youth and Family Work Journal*, 44: 77–93.

McLaughlin, H. (2009) 'Keeping service user involvement in research honest', *British Journal of Social Work*, 40(5): 1591–608.

McLeod, A.J. (2000) *Listening but Not Hearing: Barriers to Effective Communication Between Young People in Public Care and Their Social Workers*, Lancaster: University of Lancaster.

McLeod, A.J. (2006) 'Respect or empowerment: alternative understandings of "listening" in childcare social work', *Adoption and Fostering*, 30(4): 43–52.

Melton, G.B. (2005) 'Treating children like people: a framework for research and advocacy', *Journal of Clinical Child and Adolescent Psychology*, 34(4): 646–57.

Menzies-Lyth, I. (1988) *Containing Anxiety in Institutions: Selected Essays*, vol. 1. Free Association Books.

Merkel-Holguin, L., Schwab-Reese, L., Drury, I., Allan, H. and Hollinshead, D. (2019) 'Nothing about me without me: children and young people's experiences with family group conferences', *Child & Family Social Work*. Online

Miller, C. and McNicholl, A. (2003) *Integrating Children's Services: Issues and Practice*, London: OPM.

Minow, M. (1990) *Making all the difference: inclusion, exclusion and American Law*. Ithaca, NY: Cornell University Press.

Morris, A.S., Silk, J.S., Steinberg, L., Myers, S.S. and Robinson, L.R. (2007) 'The role of the family context in the development of emotion regulation', *Social Development (Oxford, England)*, 16(2): 361–88, doi: 10.1111/j.1467-9507.2007.00389.

Morris, K., White, S., Doherty, P. and Warwick, L. (2015) 'Out of time: theorizing family in social work practice', *Child & Family Social Work*, 22: 51–60.

Morrison, T. (2005) *Staff Supervision in Social Care* (3rd edn), Brighton: Pavilion.

Muench, K., Diaz, C. and Wright, R. (2017) 'Children and parent participation in child protection conferences: a study in one English local authority', *Child Care in Practice*, 23(1): 49–63.

Mulcachy, L. and Lloyd-Bostock, S. (1994) 'Managers as third-party dispute handlers in complaints about hospitals', *Law and Policy*, 16: 185–208.

Mulcahy, L. and Tritter, J. (1998) 'Pyramids, pathways, and iceberg- understanding the relationship between dissatisfaction, complaints and disputes', *Sociology of Health & Illness*, 20(6): 825–47. https://doi.org/10.1111/1467-9566.00131.

Munro, E. (2001) 'Empowering looked-after children', *Child & Family Social Work*, 6: 129–37.

Munro, E. (2011) 'Munro Review of child protection: final report – a child-centred system', available from: https://www.gov.uk/government/publications/munro-review-of-child-protection-final-report-a-child-centred-system [Accessed 13 November 2017].

Munro, E. (2012) 'Munro Review of child protection: progress report', available from: https://www.gov.uk/government/publications/progress-report-moving-towards-a-child-centred-system [Accessed 13 November 2017].

Munro, E. (2016) 'Frontline Leadership Seminar – The Munro Review – what's changed and where do we go next'?, available from: http://www.communitycare.co.uk/2016/05/03/watch-eileen-munro-bureaucracy-blame-building-better-future-social-work [Accessed 28 December 2017].

Murray, C. and Hallett, C. (2000) 'Young people's participation in decisions affecting their welfare', *Childhood*, 7(1): 11–25.

Narey, M. and Owers, M. (2018) *Foster Care in England: A Review for the Department for Education*, London: HMSO, available from: https://assets.publishing.service.gov.uk/government/uploads/system/uploads/attachment_data/file/679320/Foster_Care_in_England_Review.pdf [Accessed 26 June 2018].

Neill, D. (2015) *Non-Complaining and Children in the Care System: A Socio-Legal Study of the Children Act 1989, S.26*, Bristol: Bristol University Press.

NSPCC (National Society for the Prevention of Cruelty to Children) (2013a) 'Statistics on looked after children', available from: http://www.nspcc.org.uk/Inform/resourcesforprofessionals/lookedafterchildren/statistics_wda88009.html [Accessed 14 September 2017].

NSPCC (National Society for the Prevention of Cruelty to Children) (2013b) 'Vicarious trauma: The consequences of working with abuse', available from: https://nspcc.org.uk/globalassets/documents/information-service/research-briefing-vicarious-trauma-consequences-working-with-abuse.pdf [accessed 10 March 2018].

O'Quigley, A. (2000) *Listening to Children's Views: The Findings and Recommendations of Recent Research*, York: Joseph Rowntree Foundation.

Ofsted (2010) *Children's Rights Director: Children's Care Monitor 2010*, Manchester: Ofsted.

Ofsted (2011a) 'Children on independent reviewing officers.A report of children's views by the Children's Rights Director for England', London: Ofsted, available from: http://www.ofsted.gov.uk/resources/childrens-views-independent-reviewing-officers [Accessed 1 November 2017].

Ofsted (2011b) 'Having corporate parents. A report of children's views by the children's Rights Director for England', London: Ofsted, available from: http://www.ofsted.gov.uk/resources/having-corporate-parents [Accessed 1 November 2017].

Ofsted (2011c) 'The voice of the child: learning lessons from serious case reviews', London: Ofsted, available from: http://www.ofsted.gov.uk/resources/voice-of-child-learning-lessons-serious-case-reviews [Accessed 1 November 2017].

Ofsted (2013a) *Fostering Quality Assurance and Data Forms 2012–13 First Statistical Release*, Manchester: Ofsted.

Ofsted (2013b) 'Independent reviewing officers: taking up the challenge?', London: Ofsted, available from: http://www.ofsted.gov.uk/resources/Independent-reviewing-officers-taking-up-the-challenge [Accessed 1 November 2017].

Ofsted (2015) 'Leeds City Council inspection of services for children in need of help and protection, children looked after and care leavers', London: Ofsted, available from: https://reports.ofsted.gov.uk/local-authorities/leeds [Accessed 2 January 2018].

Ofsted (2016) 'Royal Borough of Kensington and Chelsea inspection of services for children in need of help and protection, children looked after and care leavers', London: Ofsted, available from: https://reports.ofsted.gov.uk/sites/default/files/documents/local-authorityreports/kensingtonandchelsea [Accessed 2 January 2018].

Ofsted (2017) 'The Annual Report of Her Majesty's Chief Inspector of Education, Children's Services and Skills 2016/17', London: Ofsted, available from: https://www.gov.uk/government/publications/ofsted-annual-report-201617-education-childrens-services-and-skills [Accessed 29 December 2017].

Oliver, C. and Dalrymple, J. (2008) *Developing Advocacy for Children and Young People: Current Issues in Research, Policy and Practice*, London: Jessica Kingsley.

Oliver, C., Knight, A. and Candappa, M. (2006) *Advocacy for Looked After Children and Children in Need: Achievements and Challenges*, London: University of London Press.

Parry, O., Pithouse, A., Anglim, C. and Batchelor, C. (2008) ' "The tip of the ice berg": children's complaints and advocacy in Wales—an insider view from complaints officers', *British Journal of Social Work*, 38(1): 5–19.

Peckover, S., Hall, C. and White, S. (2008) 'From policy to practice: the implementation and negotiation of technologies in everyday child welfare', *Children & Society*, 23(2): 136–48.

Pert, H., Diaz, C. and Thomas, N. (2014) 'Children's participation in LAC reviews: a study in one English local authority', *Child & Family Social Work*, 22: 1–10.

Pinkney, S. (2013) 'Participation and emotions: troubling encounters between children and social welfare professionals', *Children & Society*, 25(1): 37–46.

Pithouse, A. and Crowley, A. (2007) 'Adults rule? Children, advocacy and complaints to social services', *Children & Society*, 21(3): 201–13.

Pölkki, P., Vornanen, R., Pursiainen, M. and Riikonen, M. (2012) 'Children's participation in child-protection processes as experienced by foster children and social workers', *Child Care in Practice*, 18(2): 107–25.

R v Rochdale (2008) EWHC Fam 3282.

Roberts, K. (2002) 'Exploring participation: older people on discharge from hospital', *Journal of Advanced Nursing*, 40(4): 413–20.

Roberts, L., Shelton, K., Meakings, S. and Smith, A. (2017) 'Care-leavers and their children placed for adoption', *Children and Youth Services Review*, 79(C): 355–61.

Roche, J. (1999) 'Children: rights, participation and citizenship', *Childhood*, 6: 475–93.

Roesch-Marsh, A., Gillies, A. and Green, D. (2016) 'Nurturing the virtuous circle: looked after children's participation in reviews, a cyclical and relational process', *Child & Family Social Work*, 22(2): 904–13.

Rosenbloom, D., Pratt, A. and Pearlman, L. A. (1995) 'Helpers' responses to trauma work: understanding and intervening in an organization', in B. Stamm (ed), *Secondary Traumatic Stress: Self-Care Issues for Clinicians, Researchers, and Educators*, Lutherville, MD: Sidran, pp 65–79.

Ruch, G. (2012) 'Where have all the feelings gone? Developing reflective and relationship-based management in child-care social work', *The British Journal of Social Work*, 42(7): 1315–32.

Ruch, G., Wilson, K., Lymbery, M. and Cooper, A. (2008) *Social Work: An introduction to Contemporary Practice*, New York: Pearson.

Sanders, R. and Mace, S. (2006) 'Agency policy and the participation of children and young people in the child protection process', *Child Abuse Review*, 15(2): 89–102.

Schofield, G. (2009) 'The voice of the child in family placement decision-making a developmental model', *Adoption and Fostering*, 29(1): 29–43.

Schofield, G. and Thoburn, J. (1996) *Child Protection: The Voice of the Child in Decision Making*, London: IPPR.

Schooling, E. (2016) 'Social care commentary: an environment where social work can flourish', 3 November, available from: https://www.gov.uk/government/speeches/ofsted-national-director-of-social-care-monthly-commentary-november-2016 [Accessed 2 January 2018].

Sebba, J., Berridge, D., Luke, N., Fletcher, J., Bell, K., Strand, S., Thomas, S., Sinclair, I. and O'Higgins, A. (2015) *The Educational Progress of Looked After Children in England: Linking Care and Educational Data*, Oxford: Rees Centre for Research in Fostering and Education and University of Bristol.

Selwyn, J. and Riley, S. (2015) *Children and Young People's Views on Being in Care: A Literature Review*, Bristol: University of Bristol and Coram Voice.

Selwyn, J. and Briheim-Crookall, L. (2017) 'Our lives, our care: the subjective well-being of looked after children', University of Bristol and Coram Voice, available from: https://coramvoice.org.uk/sites/default/files/1053-CV-Our-Lives-Our-Care-report5.pdf [Accessed 20 January 2019].

Shaw, I. and Gould, N. (2001) *Qualitative Research in Social Work*, London: Sage.

Sheldon, B. and Chilvers, R. (2002) 'An empirical study of the obstacles to evidence-based practice', *Social Work and Social Sciences Review*, 10: 6–26.

Shemmings, D. (2000) 'Professionals' attitudes to children's participation in decision-making: dichotomous accounts and doctrinal contents', *Child & Family Social Work*, 5: 235–44.

Shier, H. (2001) 'Pathways to participation: openings, opportunities and obligations. A new model for enhancing children's participation in decision-making, in line with Article 13.1 of the UNCRC', *Children & Society*, 15(2): 107–17.

Shoesmith, S. (2016) *Learning from Baby P: The Politics of Blame, Fear and Denial*, London: Jessica Kingsley.

Simons, K. (1995). *I Am Not into Complaining but… Complaints Procedures in Social Services Departments*, York: Joseph Rowntree Foundation.

Sinclair, R. (1998) 'Research review: involving children in planning their care', *Child & Family Social Work*, 3: 137–42.

Sinclair, R. (2004) 'Participation in practice: making it meaningful, effective and sustainable', *Children & Society*, 18: 106–18.

Smith, M., Gallagher, M., Wosu, H., Stewart, J., Cree, V.E., Hunter, S. and Wilkinson, H. (2011) 'Engaging with involuntary service users in social work: findings from a knowledge exchange project', *British Journal of Social Work*, 42(8): 1460–77.

Social Care Wales (2017) 'Code of professional practice for social care', available from: https://socialcare.wales/cms_assets/file-uploads/Code-of-Professional-Practice-for-Social-Care-web-version.pdf [Accessed 26 January 2018].

Stabler, L., O'Donnell, C., Forrester, D., Diaz, C., Willis, S. and Brand, S.L. (2019) 'Shared decision making: what is good practice in delivering meetings? Involving families meaningfully in decision-making to keep children safely at home: A rapid realist review', technical report, available from: https://whatworks-csc.org.uk/wp-content/uploads/WWCSC_Shared_Decision_Making_Rapid_Realist_Review_full_report.pdf [Accessed 20 November 2019].

Stanley, T. and Featherstone, B. (2015) 'The voice of the child within a "whole family" approach', in *The Voice of the Child: Evidence Review*, Dartington: Research in Practice.

Stewart, A. and MacIntyre, G. (2013) 'Advocacy: models and effectiveness', *Evidence Summaries to Support Social Services in Scotland. Insight 20*, IRISS, available from: https://www.iriss.org.uk/sites/default/files/iriss-insight-20.pdf [Accessed 16 January 2019].

Stevenson, L. (2018) 'Should local authorities be able to scrap the independent reviewing officer role?', *Community Care*, 20 February, available from: www.communitycare.co.uk/2018/02/20/local-authorities-able-scrap-independent-reviewing-officer-role/ [Accessed 10 January 2019].

Thoburn, J. (2010) 'Looked after children: care planning, placement choice and review', *Community Care Inform*, available from: http://www.ccinform.co.uk/articles/article.aspx?liArticleID=1548 [Accessed 17 September 2017].

Thomas, D.R. (2003) *A General Inductive Approach for Qualitative Data Analysis*, Auckland: University of Auckland.

Thomas, N. (2000) *Children, Family and the State: Decision-Making and Child Participation*, London: Macmillan.

Thomas, N. (2002) *Children, Family and the State: Decision-making and Child Participation*, Bristol: Policy Press.

Thomas, N. (2011) 'Care planning and review for looked after children: fifteen years of slow progress?', *British Journal of Social Work*, 41: 387–98.

Thomas, N. (2015) 'The voice of the child in statutory work', in *The Voice of the Child: Evidence Review*, Dartington: Research in Practice.

Thomas, N. and O'Kane, C. (1999) 'Children's participation in reviews and planning meetings when they are "looked after" in middle childhood', *Child & Family Social Work*, 4: 221–30.

Thørnblad, R., Strandbu, A., Holtan, A. and Jenssen, T. (2016) 'Family group conferences: from Maori culture to decision-making model in work with late modern families in Norway', *European Journal of Social Work*, 19(6): 992–1003.

Tickle, L. (2016) 'Can independent reviewing officers really be independent?', *The Guardian*, 20 September, available from: www.theguardian.com/social-care-network/2016/sep/20/can-independent-reviewingofficers-really-be-independent [Accessed 20 March 2018].

Tickle, L. (2018) 'Don't blame social workers. It's the system that's broken', *The Guardian*, 17 January, available from: https://theguardian.com/commentisfree/2018/jan/17/social-workers-child-protection-adoption [Accessed 26 January 2018].

Timms, J. and Thoburn, J. (2006) 'Your shout! Looked after children's perspectives on the Children Act 1989', *Journal of Social Welfare and Family Law*, 28(2): 153–70.

UNCRC (United Nations Convention on the Rights of the Child) (1989) *Convention of the Rights of the Child*, New York: United Nations.

Van Bijleveld, G.G., Dedding, C.W.M. and Bunders-Aelen, J.F.G. (2013) 'Children's and young people's participation within child welfare and child protection services: a state-of the art review', *Child & Family Social Work*, 1–10, Advance Access doi: 10.1111/cfs.12082.

Vis, S.A., Holtan, A. and Thomas, N. (2010) 'Obstacles for child participation in care and protection cases: why Norwegian social workers find it difficult', *Child Abuse Review*, 21: 21–43.

Wade, J., Biehal, N., Farrelly, N. and Sinclair, I. (2011) *Caring for Abused and Neglected Children: Making the Right Decisions for Reunification or Long-Term Care*, London: Jessica Kingsley.

Warren, L. and Cook, J. (2005) 'Working with older women in research: benefits and challenges of involvement', in L. Lowes and I. Hulatt (eds) *Involving Service Users in Health and Social Care Research*, London: Routledge, pp 171–89.

Waterhouse R. (2000) *Lost in Care: Report of the Tribunal on Inquiry into Abuse of Children in Care in the Former County Council Areas of Gwynedd and Clwydd*, London: HMSO.

Who Cares Trust (2016) 'The statistics', available from: http://www.thewhocarestrust.org.uk/pages/the-statistics.html [Accessed 14 September 2017].

Wilkins, D. (2013) 'Guide to writing transparent and deliverable plans using SMART objectives', *Community Care Inform*, available from: https://www.researchgate.net/publication/307864588_Guide_to_developing_social_work_care_plans [Accessed 23 February 2017].

Index

Note: Page numbers for figures appear in italics, 'n' after a page number indicates the endnote number

bureaucracy and 9, 12, 13, 92, 96,
     120–1, 157, 159, 162, 165, 168
burnout, fatigue, stress 3, 8, 11
care plans 98–9
Child Protection Conferences 43–4,
     53, 59, 60, 63, 157
decline in the status of 9–10
as gatekeepers 28, 114, 149
high caseloads 6–7, 11, 13, 57, 133,
     157, 166
inexperience 7, 68, 92, 95, 96–9
parents/SWs relationship 46–7, 48,
     53, 55–6, 57, 62, 63, 157
parents' views of 11–12, 56–8
pressured work environment 7–8,
     11–12, 13, 95, 155
short-term work 8, 35, 56–7, 68
social care meetings 34–5
statutory visit 91, 92, 115n1
SWs recruitment 62
SWs retention 3, 56, 62, 78, 158,
     166, 167
vicarious trauma 8
'zombie social work' 3–4, 13, 92, 93,
     94, 159
SWs/children relationship 86, 168
barriers to effective participation 89,
     157
building rapport 62, 78
children/SWs poor relationship 12,
     45, 55, 70, 76–8, 155
children's participation and 65, 155
children's views of SWs 54–6,
     75–9
high turnover of SWs 35, 56–7, 62,
     67, 68, 69–72, 75, 78, 89, 96–9,
     109, 111, 118, 155, 161
importance of children/SWs good
     relationship 45, 62, 110–11,
     157–8, 162
meeting children alone 61
SW's personal attributes 72, 75–6,
     109
SWs on participation 12, 163
lack of understanding of
     'participation' 12, 89, 99–101,
     117, 155, 164
paternalistic approach 105, 158,
     163
protecting children vs promoting
     participation 28, 114, 158
theory/practice disconnection
     12–13, 100–1, 106, 133, 160,
     168–9

T
teachers 50, 92, 102, 103, 159
technical rational approach 131–2, 165
theory: 'espoused theory'/'theory in use'
     101, 106, 160, 168
Thomas, N.
     Climbing Wall of Participation 22
'tick box' culture 26, 106, 110
Tickle, Louise ix–x, 167
tokenism (tokenistic participation) 12,
     26, 45, 92, 156, 164
advocates 156
Arnstein's ladder of participation 19,
     20
Child Protection Conferences 45,
     49–50, 51, 59, 61, 63
CiC reviews 80, 86, 100, 104–5, 134
SMs 130, 131
twin-tracking 98, 115n2

U
UK (United Kingdom) 31
     Child Protection Conferences 43
     children's participation 29
UNCRC (United Nations Convention
     on the Rights of the Child) 4–5,
     27, 100, 155
     Article 12: 5, 29, 31
     on children's participation 5, 25, 29,
     31, 44, 155
     participation, definition of 16–17
US (United States) 31

V
Victoria Climbié Inquiry (2001) 6

W
Wales 5, 6, 7
     Waterhouse Report 140, 153
wealth disparities 7
wilful blindness 3, 121, 160

Printed in Great Britain
by Amazon

66452602R00118